# Out-of-School Tales of a Reluctant Educator

## What people are saying about

### *Out-of-School Tales of a Reluctant Educator:*

*We learn to teach in fragmented, layered ways. Rarely does a master teacher unpack her wisdom with such respect for her craft and her readers. This funny, bittersweet, provocative telling of a life fully lived, while immersed in the lives of young people, honors teachers as well as learners. Page gets it—the "it" that Paul Goodman wrote is the grace, discrimination, and response to students, for whom education is an art. I relived my own teaching as I read and re-read these stories. Funny, irreverent at times, but always compelling; Page provides a new yardstick for measuring educational success.*
–Daniel Thompson, Director of CIFE: Curriculum and Instruction Field Experiences, The Pennsylvania State University

*A fun read especially for anyone familiar with schools. Authentically and courageously written. Marilyn discloses how she bravely and creatively persisted through surprising ordeals in the education of both students and herself.*
–Alice Faulkner Barrow, Former Elementary School Teacher; Computer Programmer Analyst, Retired

*... writing is brilliant, funny, fresh, irreverent.*
–Jeannie Page, Director of Client Services; Motivational Speaker and Writer

*'Out-of-School Tales of a Reluctant Educator' is an enjoyable and amusing story about a teacher's journey sharing 40 years of current events with her classroom. Page was able to take us through her growth as an educator, the growth of her students, and even the growth of the country through these events. Whether she thought she wanted to be or not, Page is an educator. I loved the huge moments in history where there were no words (President Kennedy, the Challenger Shuttle, 9/11); they were moving.*
–Mike Epstein, Stay-at-Home Dad

*Through Marilyn's humorous and insightful story as a 'Reluctant Educator,' we gain a deeper understanding of both the American education system and our own personal journeys through it. She combines the political subtext and analysis of Jonathan Kozol with the heartwarming humility of Annie Lamott. What a wonderful course of study to join her on.*
–Carmen D'Arcangelo, Autobiographical Fiction Writer and Coach; Consultant; Author, *Grace* in Anthology, *We Came to Say*


*'Ms. Page to the office, Ms. Page to the office, NOW!' Though Marilyn Page's accidental career in teaching spans many more years than even the most reluctant of students, her calls to the office as a subject of scrutiny averages just a little bit higher than many of her hormone-addled scholars. But don't be mistaken! This is a good thing, as Page was a teacher who questioned bad policy and pushed for change well in synch with cultural shifts rocking the nation. This is the story of a reluctant teacher who became an excellent teacher, a teacher who discovered self-empowerment makes not only for more engaged students, but better teachers as well. A very interesting and enjoyable read. But why am I left with the feeling I would have been dragged OUT of Ms. Page's classroom by the ear?*
–William Meyer, Product Manager

## Out-of-School Tales of a Reluctant Educator

... is a brilliant, insightful, vivid, heartwarming narrative of a reluctant teacher's attempt to navigate the sometimes treacherous and rollicking waters of adolescence.

A week after Dr. Martin Luther King Jr. gave his stirring *I Have a Dream* speech on the National Mall to the thousands who had joined the March on Washington for Jobs and Freedom, Marilyn Monks Page started her first teaching job at Milltown High School in Milltown, MA. A presidential assassination and a host of civil-rights marches, sit-ins, protests, and conflicts provided the backdrop for the launching of her accidental career as an educator.

Page had never wanted to be a teacher. She was out of work, there was a teacher shortage, Milltown High School needed a teacher, and the rest is history. She had no training, no coursework, knew nothing about adolescents, and, besides teaching world history and American geography, she was charged to teach first and second year Spanish even though she could barely speak a word. *Out-of-School Tales of a Reluctant Educator* spans forty-two years of poignant, unexpected, sometimes scary, and mostly hilarious events that will leave you laughing; the adolescent escapades might remind you of your own. At the same time, woven throughout is a portrait of how a teacher develops her ability to teach.

It's all here—experiences in all kinds of schools in inner-city, rural, and suburban districts in different parts of the country with different kinds of students, different kinds of colleagues, and different kinds of administrators—and all this within an historical context. From Billy giving her a very strange gift that he had crafted in shop class, to Page joining her neighbors in chasing two fat pigs down a country road in Vermont, there isn't a dull moment. It's history, it's sociology, it's education, and it's all about adolescents. It might make you laugh; it might even make you cry a little.

# OUT-OF-SCHOOL TALES

# OF A RELUCTANT EDUCATOR

----------------

## MARILYN MONKS PAGE

## FOREWORD BY BRUCE A. MARLOWE

### COVER ILLUSTRATION AND DESIGN BY ANNIE KANE O'CONNOR

Disclaimer: Events and people are real. Most names of places and people are pseudonyms to protect privacy. Where there is a composite, in the form of a person or of an event, there is no impact on the veracity or substance. Others may remember these events differently. That is the nature of memory and a function of each reader's perceptual lenses.

Pollywog Pond Press, a division of Warrington Press

San Francisco, CA

Printed in the United States of America

ISBN-10: 0-615-93217-7

ISBN-13: 978-0-615-93217-0

Cover illustration and design by Annie Kane O'Connor

## ABOUT THE AUTHOR

Marilyn Monks Page grew up in Worcester, MA and lived, and raised her children, in the Boston area for many years. She began her career as a high school social-studies and Spanish teacher and taught in every grade 7 through 12, at every academic level, in rural, suburban, and urban school systems in different parts of the United States. She taught at the university level and worked with pre- and in-service teachers, grades K–12, for 20 years. Page also directed a research project for the development of K–12 professional certification requirements in the state of Washington. She has been the technology coordinator for education programs at two universities and developed the first middle-school, teacher-preparation programs in the Vermont State College System. She earned her EdD from the University of Massachusetts in Amherst in Instructional Leadership and in Educational Media and Technology. She is the author, and author with Bruce A. Marlowe, of several books. At any given time you can find her in Boston or in San Francisco or in Seattle or in Paris. And she likes it that way.

Contact Marilyn at www.marilynmonkspage.com

## ABOUT THE ILLUSTRATOR/DESIGNER

Annie Kane O'Connor grew up in Groton, Massachusetts and earned her BFA from the Massachusetts College of Art and Design in Boston. She went on to receive her teaching license in art education from St. Michael's College in Colchester, Vermont and, after a bit of wandering around the country, returned to Boston to earn her master's in art education, again at MassArt. She is an art teacher with the Lexington Public School System and a freelance illustrator and painter. She lives in Waltham, MA with her husband Tony, and when not working in her studio, she can be found running along the Charles River, working in her garden, or in her living room watching *Law and Order SVU*.

Contact Annie at www.anniekaneoconnor.com

# Contents

-------------------------------------------------------------------------------

## Abbreviations and Acronyms

| | |
|---|---|
| AV | audiovisual |
| EST | Eastern Standard Time |
| EPA | Environmental Protection Agency |
| GPS | global positioning system |
| HD | History Day |
| IEP | Individualized Education Program |
| JFK | John F. Kennedy |
| MIA | missing-in-action |
| NASA | National Aeronautics and Space Administration |
| NHD | National History Day |
| OCD | obsessive-compulsive disorder |
| UMASS | University of Massachusetts |
| UPS | United Parcel Service |

# Acknowledgements

Thank you to every student, student-teacher, teacher, librarian, administrator, colleague, and professor who crossed my path. I learned something from every one of you. A very, very special thanks goes to Bruce A. Marlowe, a colleague and friend without equal, who is one of the most skilled, intelligent, and caring educators I know. Thanks, Bruce, for being so kind and so darn funny and for agreeing to write the *Foreword*. No one else could have done it.

Thank you, Annie Kane O'Connor, for brilliantly illustrating and designing the book's cover. Annie, working with you was an absolute joy. You are a genius of an illustrator and a delight as a person.

A most important thank you goes to Dad, who never met an adventure he didn't love, who always took chances, who was often naughty in wonderful and uproarious ways, who always quickly and willingly supported any way-out ideas I came up with, and who taught me to relish the journey. His story-telling, his singing (especially of *Hinky Dinky Parley-Vous*), his pranks, his outrageous sagas, his toaster that shot the burned bread across the room, his clock whose hands went backwards, and his laughter are legendary; just ask his grandchildren. His effervescent demeanor was contagious and lives on. Everyone should have a Dad in his life.

Thank you to my three fabulous children, Dave, Phil, and Jeannie, who are the most independent and most independent-thinking people I know. Their caring, compassion, and support know no bounds. You are forever in my heart.

Thank you to the people at CreateSpace.com who answered quickly and with expertise. Everyone was open, never made me feel foolish, and helped me find answers to my questions.

Thank you to the reviewers who graciously and willingly gave their time to read the book, ask questions, and write comments. They represent different professions, different locations, and different age groups. Thank you (in alphabetical order), Alice Faulkner Barrow, Carmen D'Arcangelo, Mike Epstein, William Meyer, Jeannie Page, and Dan Thompson.

# Dedication

To Allan, without whom my high school days would not have been half as much fun. You left us way too soon and we can never repay you for your service. You are not forgotten. Rest in peace, Allan.

To Joan, who was always ready to help a friend and used her twinkling eyes brilliantly for all sorts of things. Rest in peace, Joan.

To Marion, who knew how to get the most out of life and always knew what she was doing. Rest in peace, Marion.

To Dr. Robert H. Ferrell, who, through his extraordinary sense of, and concern for, the well-being of his students, taught me that there is a whole lot more to teaching than teaching. Thank you for being in my life, Dr. Ferrell.

To Big-Brother Norm, who, along with Dad, made our growing-up home a rousing, raucous, wickedly priceless place to live. You taught me so many things, especially after you sprayed my hair with shaving cream as I was getting ready for a date. That is when I learned to always lock the bathroom door. It was a good thing to learn. Thank you for having a heart as big as the world and for always being there for anyone who needs you.

To Mom, who has always held down the fort and who has taken care of her children better than anyone, anywhere, and at age ninety-eight, still does. Mom, thank you.

To Gerry, who brightens every day.

And to the future: Alia, Violet, Aria, Brendan, and Gwenna

*I do not approve of anything that tampers with natural ignorance. Ignorance is like a delicate exotic fruit; touch it and the bloom is gone. The whole theory of modern education is radically unsound. Fortunately, in England, at any rate, education produces no effect whatever. If it did, it would prove a serious danger to the upper classes, and probably lead to acts of violence in Grosvenor Square.*

—Lady Bracknell in Oscar Wilde

*The Importance of Being Ernest*

# Foreword

*Any fool can make history, but it takes a genius to write it.*

—Oscar Wilde

This is a story with plenty of fools. But, make no mistake; there is real genius here too. I am getting ahead of myself.

It's 1992. A new job, a new part of the country. Everything is unfamiliar. I am in a poorly lit elevator in an aging building at a small state college in rural Vermont. The air is dank. The indoor-outdoor carpeting beneath my feet is wet, stained with mud and melting snow. A new colleague, Marilyn Page, is with me; she is still unfamiliar, unusual too. There is a curious mixture here. She has a no-nonsense mien, a somewhat skeptical expression, but there is a wry smile and a twinkle in her eye. For some reason I can no longer remember, we are transporting a very large television set on an over-sized, top-heavy cart from the top to the ground floor. Moments after the doors close, the elevator begins its slow descent. Then suddenly, we stop between floors, the elevator straining to move. Soon, the elevator begins to shake violently. We begin to rock back and forth, but we are no longer descending.

There is much to be learned in moments like these ...

As I was soon to discover, Marilyn relishes a good adventure, which is a good thing, as her life story reads like a mythic quest. In this powerful, painfully honest, and at times, absolutely hilarious chronicle, we are taken places intimate and social, personal and political. In many ways, Marilyn's memoir is the story of America from the early 1960s to the present, a history that includes as backdrop the appalling tragedy of Vietnam, alongside the triumphs, struggles, pain and dissonance of the Civil Rights Movement. But even the grimmest of tales told here—of urban blight and crushing poverty, of state-sanctioned abuse, of institutionalized bigotry and sexism, of environmental degradation and corporate malfeasance, all of these tales—are told with such tremendous gusto, savvy and wit that Marilyn is able to inoculate the reader from this painful past well

enough for us to consider the larger lessons she so cogently illus-
trates.

Marilyn expertly weaves together the story of her own coming of
age with incisive observation about a time period characterized so
often in ways that seem hackneyed and agonizingly cliché. In con-
trast, there is a freshness, a vitality, and an immediacy to this memoir. Marilyn's remarkable candor about her own fallibility, about
her fears and her inadequacies, about the very real needs of her students, about the challenges of ordinary people trying to make sense
of very confusing times—all serve to humanize this era. She brings
to mind, with equally evocative prose, images of demonstrations in
the street, halls teeming with adolescents, and the inner life of a
teacher worrying about the inner lives of young people, their learning, their engagement in the world. From the very first pages, the
reader is drawn into not one but several richly layered, highly personal stories of lived experience, which, almost on every page, are
deftly woven together with trenchant social commentary.

Mostly though, this is a teacher's tale. Marilyn's classroom career
begins just one week after Martin Luther King, Jr. proclaimed, "1963
is not an end, but a beginning." She is hired to teach Spanish, world
history, and geography. When she starts, she speaks little Spanish,
is still months from earning her teaching certificate, while the nation is almost a whole year away from prohibiting the segregation of
lunch counters and movie theaters. She is initiated into the profession before teachers' unions, before it was illegal for superinten-
dents to demand that female teachers remain unmarried, before
teachers were allowed to talk about race and inequality, about bigotry, poverty, and social justice. Unprepared, in any official capacity,
she struggles to figure out, as Alfie Kohn might say, what to do *to*
students, as the common wisdom of the time indicated. Then slowly, after careful observation, honest self-appraisal and enormous
effort, she recognizes a common humanity within the classroom
walls and the importance of working *with* students as she powerful-
ly engages them with the unfolding history of which they are a part.

When she began this most demanding of professions, Marilyn,

was, as she says, an "accidental teacher." How refreshing, in our current age of rigid standards, scripted curricula, and teacher accountability, where states routinely insist that teachers be "highly qualified," to hear such an accomplished educator say out loud what every teacher secretly fears, yet furtively knows to be true: "I have no idea what I am doing."

... The moment in the elevator revealed to me a person who was to become a lifelong friend. As I soon came to find out, by the time I was alone with her in that Vermont State College elevator in 1992, Marilyn had already been teaching for many years. And although she would profess otherwise, I already knew, standing there in those close and clammy quarters that behind her wry smile, behind the twinkle in her eyes, was a wealth of experience and wisdom. This recognition did nothing to assuage my more immediate concern however, as the elevator, while still shaking violently, began to emit an awful, screeching sound which filled the small space, and slowly began to crescendo—Marilyn and I exchanged silent glances: I wide-eyed with alarm, she bemused—and then, abruptly, there was an incredibly loud "pop" and our descent continued.

When we reach the ground floor, I sigh with relief. Marilyn rolls with laughter. It was as if she had just stepped off a fantastic amusement park ride. Apparently, the elevator doors on the top floor closed on the electric cord hanging from the television set. The cord had stretched and strained until it finally snapped, releasing the elevator car so that it could continue its descent. This simple, mundane explanation did nothing to diminish my sense of relief ... or Marilyn's evident delight.

This delight in possibility, in wondering how things will unfold, in recounting how they did unfold in classrooms over a span of more than forty years, is palpable in every chapter of this wonderful gem of a memoir.

Enjoy.

—*Bruce A. Marlowe, PhD*, Professor of Educational Psychology and Special Education; Roger Williams University, Bristol, RI

# Prologue

I was one of those kids who knew from an early age what I wanted to be—and that was a social worker or a missionary. But everyone kept telling me that I ought to be a teacher. Not that that was anything unusual given the times. It was actually considered progressive thinking and, by many, to be a step up from the job or calling of housewife. No thank you to the teaching, I would tell them; I know where I am going and it isn't there. Regardless, life can play tricks on us. Life had something other than social work in mind for me.

It is many years ago. I am standing in the kitchen of my very warm, fun, sometimes noisy and riotous (mostly because of my older brother Norm), rather crowded, soon-to-be-seven-person, understated, New-England-cottage-with-the-front-porch kind of childhood home, a home in which Mom was born. It's a place where every week, Mom drags out the old washing machine, plops it in the middle of the kitchen floor, throws in the wash, runs the machine, asks me to put everything through the wringer, and then sends me outside to hang everything on the line that stretches across the yard to the back fence. Out there in the winter, without fail, each piece of laundry freezes as solid as a board and swings like an old storm window in the wind. I don't really mind doing this; in fact, I kind of like it. And now that I have finished that job this morning, here, in this laundering kitchen, I am waiting for Dad, whose bigger-than-life character takes up quite a bit of metaphysical space in our home. He and I are going, for lack of a better phrase, investigative slumming.

"Dad, are you ready?" I ask.

"I'm ready!" Dad proclaims vigorously to me and to anyone else within earshot. He is always loud—happily, boisterously loud. He heads for the back door, grabs his tan jacket and says in a singsongy way, "Off we go in a cloud of dust, just like a herd of turtles."

That was Dad-speak for *let's go* and that same scene repeated itself every Saturday morning as Dad and I set off for the city's worst run-down neighborhoods. I wanted to study the poverty, the hope-lessness, the people. Who lives there? Why do they live there? How did they get there? Why are they so poor? Why doesn't somebody do something? Dad never hesitated. I thought he was as interested as I was. He was always helping someone. There were his grocery shopping trips for the senior citizens, the home visitations with the sick, and his endless work on fundraisers. Maybe he was looking for his next great cause.

Or maybe his willingness was something else entirely. It could have been that these impoverished and dilapidated areas were next to *Jew Town,* as Worcester residents affectionately called the area around Water Street. I was ten. I thought *Jew Town* was an ordinary town like West Boylston or Shrewsbury or Holden. There in the middle of the ugly blight was an oasis of the world's best bakeries and delicatessens, and on weekend mornings, people wrapped around the block waiting in line to get the fabulous goodies. The luscious aroma of baking bread, like no other smell in the world, wafted everywhere, somehow pulling us in after our drive-by re-search.

Maybe the trip to the bakeries and the do-good study of destitu-tion were linked somehow. After all, an important study at the Uni-versity of Southern Brittany in France in 2012, found that inhaling the aroma of freshly-baked bread can make you a kinder, more be-nevolent person. Then again, Dad bought a loaf of rye bread every trip, and by the time we got home, he would have ripped off the end of the loaf and eaten it already. Maybe he was just hungry.

These investigative trips were my first studies in the field of so-cial work. During these expeditions, I would look in awe at the top-pling trash heaps outside the bedraggled buildings, and, if doors were open, I would ask that we stop so I could look up the stairways or into the forlorn entryways where I would gawk at more junk; peeling paint; sometimes a comatose drunk; a broken baby carriage; a banged-up, stolen, grocery cart; and, further in, the creepy dark-ness. These tours lasted about an hour. After I had my fill of misery and the downtrodden, and after the purchase of rye, and once in a while pumpernickel, bread, we would return home. I would be more determined than ever to do something about these living conditions and to help the people in them. I was going to be a social worker and save the world, or at least some of her people. Maybe I would be a missionary and go to Africa and save *her* people.

I hated Boston University. Dad didn't think girls needed to go to college in the first place. When he told me that, I knew for sure that the slum exploration had been all about the bread. I wasn't deterred, but I had just turned seventeen and the huge city campus was daunting. Worse, the experience there caused me to suffer from grade stress disorder. I had been second in my high school graduating class with a grade point average of 4.0. I had even skipped a grade in elementary school and half a grade in high school. At Boston University, my grade point average always hovered pathetically around the 2.3 marker. Suddenly everyone was smarter than I was. It felt awful. It felt oppressive, stifling, unfair. In a matter of months, I went from being the invincible academic queen of my little kingdom to being a colossal dunce in an immense, unfamiliar, uninviting land.

I didn't feel at all at home there. Sometime around December, I noticed a lot of new posters everywhere. I couldn't figure out what they were advertising. *Happy Chanukah* the signs broadcast. What is *Chanukah*, and how do you pronounce *Chanukah*, anyway? I guessed it must be Chan (as in Charlie)-U-kah. I doubted I would ever need to use the word in a sentence, but I was curious. Although I didn't want to miss a good party, I decided to ignore the notices; they didn't even divulge the time and place of the shindig. It was probably just one of those fraternity things.

Aside from these negatives, I did love sociology. Every day I was more fascinated by what I was learning than I had been the day before. I was definitely in the right field. What could be more intriguing or useful than studying society and all her components? Do social structures such as ethnicity, class, religion, and gender determine and limit an individual's behavior or do individuals have and make free choices which influence social systems? How do institutions impact the features of a society? How does society determine institutions? How do time frames affect social patterns? And how does getting answers to these questions change society? Can answers change society? I couldn't get enough. I was like a bloated, porous sponge that never got full. Who cared that this was one of the few areas open to women at the time. I didn't.

Studying wasn't the only thing I was doing. When I was nineteen and still an undergraduate, I married my handsome and devilishly charming Sailor Man whom I had met two years earlier while out on a double date with someone else. Karma, the ever vigilant shrew who is always meddling in people's lives, would eventually punish me for this crisscross. Meanwhile, I showed off handsome and devilishly charming Sailor Man, paraded him around campus, and thought, "Ha, see what I have," and before too long, I joined the rather crowded club of young women putting their husbands through school.

I got a job with the impressive title of assistant psychiatric social worker in what was then called the State School for Retarded. One responsibility was to conduct an intake interview with each new resident's parent(s) or guardian(s). I would do this while the psychologist was simultaneously administering the necessary psychological and intelligence placement tests to the new arrival. I would record as much of this person's background as possible. When the ancestral history was not available, I would begin the interview with the pre-natal experience and follow life events up to the present. The accuracy of the reporting depended on who was *doing* the reporting. Very often, the information came from a social worker or a foster parent or a police officer; less often, it was from one or both of the parents.

Given what I heard in these interviews, it was a challenge to keep myself on an even keel. The incest, the brutality, the abuse, the neglect, the genetics, and for some, just an incident of birth when something had gone wrong. No matter what the story, we put as many matching names as we could on the *Family Tree of Retardation*. The banner blasting this caption spread proudly and forever from one corner of the room to another. Under the heading, the sprawling, Halloween-like, scary tree—with too many branches to count—stretched from floor to ceiling, from wall to wall. We had to shift things to fit new entries.

What I remember about that tree, besides its size and location, is that it started with two people, one man, one woman, who had come into western Massachusetts from Canada in the late 1800s. The man's surname was Fank. And there were Fanks all over the branches. I had to look at that monstrosity every time I sat at my desk. Even until the present, I cannot meet anyone named Fank without wondering and wanting to ask, "How did you escape the lineage?" Or, alternatively, "Did you?" My thinking was becoming warped. The names of the birth-trauma people, and any others who had no apparent connection to the *tree-of-retardation* people, went into a pile for future trees. At some point, the reasoning went, we would probably find familial-retardation  connections for all of them.

For the second part of the job I made home visits to gather more information and to determine whether or not the environment was safe enough for residents to have brief vacations. The best part of that mission was that I got to drive through the beautiful country-side of the Berkshires. The places I visited, though, were not always as attractive. They held the same range of stories as did the intake interviews. There were shacks; there were trailers; there were Quonset huts; there were middle-class homes; there were beautiful homes; there were ghetto homes; there were neat homes, clean homes, hoarding homes, filthy homes, crowded homes. Many of the homes' inhabitants would probably have fit the intellectual range the State School served. The small minority of the domiciles that were in upscale areas often belonged to foster families or to families whose children had suffered birth injuries or had chromosomal ir-regularities such as Down syndrome. Most of the State School resi-dents never got to make home visits, either because the home condi-tions were deplorable or no relative or guardian ever asked.

The third piece of my job involved trips to stores. I would take the higher functioning men and women on these jaunts. Hopefully, the logic was, these men and women, always on separate gender trips, could learn and practice living skills such as buying items; counting money; figuring out change; and, most important, making decisions. Almost always, the outsiders with whom we came in contact thought we were all one big leaderless group, all one and the same, all strange, all speaking in funny voices that didn't sound quite right, all looking peculiar, all roaming around clueless. Sometimes I corrected the gawkers, sometimes I didn't. I learned more if I pretended to be one of the bunch.

I remember several highlights of that State-School, social-work job. I remember that for the home visits in dangerous areas the school required me to first stop at the local police station and request a police escort. On one of those occasions, I was in a hurry and neglected to do that. I drove into a crowded, ugly, forsaken, risky section of the city; parked the car; got out; looked around apprehensively; walked down a dirty alley; and then climbed up the creaking back wooden stairs to the second floor of a shabby, dilapidated, three-decker. I knocked on the door. There was no answer. I turned the door knob and pushed the unlocked door open. There were piles and piles of disheveled clothes everywhere on the floor, and drug paraphernalia covered three tables. There was no other furniture in that room and I wasn't about to check out any other part of the apartment. I hightailed it out of there, flew down the rickety stairs, scurried through the cluttered alley, jumped in my car, and took off. I was lucky that I didn't encounter anyone in there. I could have been robbed; I could have been raped; I could have been shot; I could have been stabbed. I never went alone again. I stamped *denied* on the vacation request.

I remember my first excursion to a drugstore with five of the School's women. They were enjoying themselves roaming up and down the aisles, looking at everything, and chatting happily when, seemingly out of nowhere, the store manager came over to us and shepherded us into his office. He accused all of us of shoplifting. I wasn't, but they apparently were, and he thought we were all in cahoots together. The five women had been stuffing all kinds of products into their coats. The objects were things they didn't need and would never use; the women liked them, so they took them. So much for the residents learning everyday skills.

On site, I remember the IQ-based, resident classifications. These designations were *moron, imbecile, and idiot* in descending order of brain, physical, emotional, social, and physiological function. I didn't pay much attention to the labels; I had seen them before in the abnormal-psychology books. But I did start to use them way too frequently in talking about, or to, people in general. I needed to stop doing that.

I remember, also, the anguish of the family who had taken in a ten-year-old foster child who, a short time after moving in with them, sexually assaulted their five-year-old daughter. The boy became one of our residents. I remember that freezing winter day when I had to drive to the far end of the State School's property on an errand and saw naked men, in the cold, roaming around in a fenced-in yard in front of Building K. My director informed me that these adult residents couldn't wear clothes because they would eat them. I remember the moaning I could hear wherever I went on the grounds. There was always an explanation.

And, without doubt, I remember that tree. That awful, dehumanizing, grotesque, macabre, freaky, obnoxious *tree*.

This is not what I had had in mind when I thought about social work. My Saturday morning missions with Dad had not prepared me for any of this. Boston University had not prepared me for any of this. Louise Meir, my boss and twenty-year employee at the State School, had not prepared me for any of this. Since no part of my job involved my going into the resident buildings, it would be eight years after I had stopped working there, that I would discover disturbing things had been going on, and continued to exist, inside those walls. James Shanks, in his series "The Tragedy of Belchertown," in the *Springfield Union* in March of 1970, described alleged horrific conditions, not the least of which were inhuman overcrowding and neglect. Except for the naked adults in the fenced-in area of Building K, I never saw anything like what I read in his reports.

Why had I been so oblivious? I guess I had been too busy interviewing parents and guardians, meandering into drug havens, being an alleged accessory to shoplifting, and driving through the countryside checking out homes for prospective visits. Evidently, I hadn't had the time or the urgent need to know what was going on *inside* the school. Unbeknown to me, I had been dancing around purgatory. It would take parental complaints, state investigations, several law suits, more exposés and a complete rethinking of how to best care for people with developmental disorders and challenges before the State School finally closed in 1992.

While I was working at the State School, there was the small incident in my personal life when one morning as I waited for the State School's carpool van, Greasy Man approached me on the sidewalk outside my thirty-five-dollar-a-month apartment above the bank and warned me that if my handsome and devilishly charming Sailor Man did not pay his ten-thousand-dollar gambling debt by such-and-such a date, there probably would be an unfortunate accident on my way to work one day. Karma had come to town.

After a year of experiencing absolutely nothing I had bargained for in either my job or my marriage and encountering everything that stunned and traumatized me, there needed to be a change of plans. First it was time to repair the crippled marriage. But after a quick and fruitless nine months in Arizona, where things were supposed to get better, where Sailor Man was in graduate school and still into shenanigans and chicanery, and where a salesman at my car-dealer employer's told me I had the figure of a brick shithouse, I called it quits. I abandoned Sailor Man and all of my belongings, jumped on the next Greyhound bus headed for New England, and spent the next three days and nights covering my head in a towel trying to escape the stinking cigar smoke on that bus. It was 1963. People smoked on buses. I arrived back home penniless; desperate; disillusioned; jobless; and reeking of, and wheezing from, that ghastly, noxious, disgusting cigar smoke. Once I got that foul odor out of my clothes, out of my nose, out of my hair, it was time for a new life, a new career.

What could I do? If not social work, what? The 1960s was such a tumultuous decade what with civil-rights marches and the war in Vietnam and burned bras and communal-living arrangements and tripped-out hippies and Andy Warhol's can of soup and Betty Fried-an's *The Feminine Mystique* and tragic assassinations and Star Trek and the Beatles and free love and Arlo Guthrie's *Alice's Restaurant Massacree* and the moon landing. It was also the time of a tremen-dous teacher shortage. And I needed a job.

Milltown High School needed a teacher for two Spanish courses, two world-history courses, and one geography course. I didn't have certification in anything and had never had an education course. Never mind education, I had never even had a course in geography, except maybe back in the fifth grade. But I had had two years of college Spanish and three years of college history courses. "I guess I can do it," I thought tentatively, not quite believing it, and with a sense of acquiescing to something I didn't want in the first place. I really needed a job, any job. Milltown, in her urgency, apparently concluded that I could do it, or, on second thought, maybe there wasn't any other candidate. Milltown hired me on a waiver for this gerrymandered schedule with the agreement that the first six months would count as student teaching and I would take courses toward certification at the same time I was teaching.

On August 28, 1963, while I was wracking my brain trying to fig-ure out what in the world I was going to do in a week on the first day of classes, I was watching Dr. Martin Luther King, Jr., on TV, as he was speaking in front of the Lincoln Memorial to the quarter mil-lion who had come by foot, on buses, on trains, and in cars to join The Civil Rights March on Washington for Jobs and Freedom and who now crammed and flooded onto the National Mall. They had come to put pressure on Congress to pass President Kennedy's Civil Rights Act that called for an end to segregation in schools by the end of the year; an end to segregation in public restaurants, theaters, hotels and at all private facilities that served the public; and an end to discriminatory and unfair employment practices. "Pass the bill! Pass the bill! Pass the bill!" they were screaming.

I listened as Dr. King said,

> *Fivescore years ago, a great American in whose symbolic shadow we stand today, signed the Emancipation Proclamation. This momentous decree came as a great beacon light of hope to millions of negro slaves who had been seared in the flames of withering injustice. ... But one hundred years later, the Negro still is not free; one hundred years later, the life of the Negro is still sadly crippled by the manacles of segregation and the chains of discrimination; one hundred years later, the Negro lives on a lonely island of poverty in the midst of a vast ocean of material prosperity; one hundred years later, the Negro is still languished in the corners of American society and finds himself in exile in his own land. ...*
>
> *Nineteen sixty-three is not an end, but a beginning. And those who hope that the Negro needed to blow off steam and will now be content, will have a rude awakening if the nation returns to business as usual. There will be neither rest nor tranquility in America until the Negro is granted his citizenship rights. ...*
>
> *I have a dream today. ... I have a dream today. ...*

I knew exactly how I was going to start the geography and history classes that first day. Dr. King's speech would be front and center. For the Spanish class, I was still endlessly practicing in front of an unforgiving mirror, "Me llamo Señorita Christen." "Me llamo Señorita Christen." "Me llamo Señorita Christen," and "¿Cómo se llama?" or should I say "¿Cómo te llamas?" and "¿Cómo ésta?" or should I say, "¿Cómo éstas?" I didn't know.

A week later, I walked up the front steps of Milltown High School, scared out of my mind, and praying I could have one twit the courage of those people who had joined the March on Washington and a sliver of the fortitude of those for whom the marchers marched.

By the end of my first year at Milltown High School, reluctantly, accidentally, and through the back door, I had become a certified, secondary-school, social-studies teacher in the state of Massachusetts. I had never wanted to be a teacher. Never, ever, ever.

# PART I

## *THE BEGINNING*

Marilyn Monks Page

# Chapter I
# Initiation

Eleven days after the start of school, just eighteen days after Dr. Martin Luther King Jr. had delivered his speech to the thousands on The National Mall in Washington, a bomb thrown from a passing car exploded in the 16th Street Baptist Church in Birmingham, Alabama and killed four fourteen-year-olds in their Sunday-School class. This triggered more violence that day: Police killed a black teenager who had been stoning cars and didn't obey their command to halt; and a group of whites murdered a black thirteen-year-old riding his bike in an area north of the city. There was no shortage of news to integrate into my classes. And who could have predicted what would happen in November.

"President Kennedy has been shot!" the voice on the loudspeaker boomed. It was 1:35 p.m. EST on November 22, 1963. I had been teaching for about two and a half months and I had no idea what to do. I was frozen, stuck to the floor as if my feet were in cement. I couldn't move; I couldn't speak. Like millions of others do, I remember exactly where I was when President Kennedy was shot; I was at the front of my classroom looking at thirty students who were looking back at me. I can't remember what I did, if anything at all, but just as school was ending, the invisible voice returned and wailed, "President Kennedy is dead." There was a very long pause and then, "School is over. Make your way to the buses." There wasn't a sound; there was only silence. The world stopped.

I was learning quickly that what happened outside a school, whether it was in the neighborhood or not, impacted what happened inside the school. Yes, I was on the fast track

3

to learning just how many responsibilities, overt and covert, declared and undeclared, a teacher might have. Was I up to the challenge?

Because of overcrowding in the high school, the principal assigned me a room in the adjoining junior high school. And besides my high-school teaching load, I had four other contractual duties. At the end of each class period, I had to put pegs under the fire doors between the high school and the junior high school to hold the doors open so that students could pass freely and quickly between the buildings; I needed to check the girls' lavatories in-between classes to make sure no one was smoking; I had to raise my classroom window shades on cloudy days; and, finally, I was the chosen monitor for a cafeteria study hall.

Considering I didn't have an inkling of what I was doing with the teaching, the extra-classroom tasks, or unpredictable events, I suppose surviving that first year meant that I had had some kind of success.

But my age was a problem. I wasn't much older than most of the high-school students in my classes and I was smaller than almost all of them. So it probably wasn't surprising that one day while I was standing at the fire doors after meticulously fixing the pegs, a teacher coming from the high school into the junior-high building told me in her best authoritative (nasty) voice and contorted face, "Hurry up and get to your class; you are going to be late."

That wasn't quite as bad as the bathroom incident. It was a Wednesday (some details of trauma never leave you) and, as required, I went to check out the girls' lavatory. As I opened the door, the smoke choked and blinded me. Instantly all the toilets flushed. Down the drains went evidence and, before I could even get a breath and make out any distinct person through the deep haze, out the door dashed the junior-high girls.

But while I was checking the whole bathroom for any cigarette remnants or other evidentiary materials, another high-school teacher came into the bathroom. What was she doing in there anyway? This was *my* lav.

"What is your name?" she demanded.

"I am ... " I tried to answer.

"Come with me to the office, right now," she interrupted.

"But, ..." I tried again.

"If you are smart, you won't talk back to me. You will end up in more trouble," she threw at me. "Now, we're going to the office."

She ignored my attempt to explain who I was. Didn't she even notice that I didn't look quite like the others who roamed the halls? Begrudgingly, but obediently, I went to the office with the oversized, over-vigilant storm trooper. It seemed the best thing to do. And in the principal's office? There wasn't even an apology.

Age also played a factor in classroom management. Pretty much all one hundred and fifty of my delightful students spread over five classes thought they could play me for a fool. After all, by the time these students got to high school, they were well-versed in how to demean, attack, frighten, humiliate, and bring to tears any substitute or new teacher. They tried every trick in the book—switching seats; giving false names; acting faint; pretending they were going to throw up; dropping pens all at once on the floor; hurling coins across the room so that the landing noise was nowhere near the perpetrator; making false accusations about other students; flinging spitballs everywhere; giving ridiculous answers that could send the class into hysterics; pushing and shoving for no reason; moving the desks all over the room at any random time; and, of course, chattering nonstop. Given that I was new, young, and small, I might as well have been wearing a bull's eye.

But, both I and the students were in for a surprise. I learned. Fast. People learn quickly when survival is at stake and I learned that you can't teach if you don't have control of the classroom. I also learned that my age mattered in the eyes of the students and that the age of the students made a difference in managing them. I learned that handling thirteen-year-olds required approaches different from those required to handle sixteen-year-olds. It became clear that managing a class was rather a hoot and that as long as I could predict what foolish thing a student was likely to do, I could prevent it. I figured out that it was a preemptive and proactive activity, not a reactive one, and I discovered that I was really, really good at it. It was a game, after all, that I won over and over and over again in the classroom.

I never won the contest in the cafeteria study hall, however. There were over one hundred students in the room with approximately eight to ten students at each long cafeteria table. I might have been able to manage it if there had been another teacher in the cafeteria with me; or I might have been able to handle it if the study hall had been during a different period of the day; or I might have been able to cope if I had had a clue what I was doing.

But if I thought it was difficult on a daily basis, it was nothing compared to a day before the start of a holiday when all hell broke loose in there. The students' favorite trick was to work together as a team at a table and silently fold the legs under the table while balancing it on their laps. Then when the leader gave the signal, all together they moved their chairs back and the very long and heavy table fell with a humongous, swooshing noise and then a shocking bang onto the floor. The students soon figured out that dropping three tables simultaneously was much better than dropping one. Pandemonium ensued. While I was attending to that impressive distraction, students bolted from the room to parts unknown. They were gone for the day.

By the end of the first half of the school year, I too was skipping out of the cafeteria. Yep, I just walked out of the room when things got too wild. I left the students to fend for themselves. I felt justified. It was a grossly unfair assignment, I reasoned. And the funniest and most surprising part was that no one ever knew that I had left.

## Chapter 2

### Extra-Curricular Activities

Milltown Junior High School taught me more, and some of it was astonishing, about twelve- and thirteen-year-olds than I ever contemplated knowing or wanted to know. I didn't teach junior-high students, but every day, all day, just because my classroom was in that building, I was entangled in their lives. This was not a bad junior high school; this was not a bad school district; these were not bad kids. There was nothing unsafe about this area or about the school. Next to a large city, Milltown was a working- and lower-middle-class suburban town whose history was rooted in textile mills. Grandma Beckford, whose trademark hat materials—soft, Persian-wool fabrics and infinitely-long pheasant feathers—still sit in a box in my closet, had even been a milliner for many years at one of the town's mills. She was one of nine children, and to help her family with expenses, she had started working at the mill at age fourteen, just one year older than these students were now at Milltown Junior High School. What a difference three generations can make. Twelve- and thirteen-year-olds no longer worked in mills; they had other things to do.

There was the day that some boys emptied their bowels into the bathroom toilets, then removed the feces and smeared them all over the walls, counters, and sinks in that same bathroom. Then they trotted down the hall, more feces in hand, probably laughing uncontrollably the whole way, and did the same in the girls' room. I was disgusted; I was shocked; I was sick to my stomach. The guilty thought it was hilarious. The innocent thought it was hilarious. I wanted to vomit.

And that wasn't all that disturbed me; there were more surprises in store for my unsuspecting and wet-behind-the-ears self. Like most junior-high schools, at Milltown, there were plenty of extra-curricular activities, all meant to enhance student growth and development and to foster healthy social interaction. Besides the usual after-school clubs, teams, and organizations, there appeared to be a purple-knee-sock group of some kind. I didn't know what they did or what their purpose was, but I also didn't care that much. I just began to notice that, on Thursdays, some of the junior-high girls wore purple knee socks.

This was the 1960s and a time of strict school dress codes for both students and teachers. Young men had to be squeaky-clean; they had to be clean-shaven; and they had to have their shirts tucked into their belted pants. No sneakers allowed. Girls could not wear slacks, as pants were called in those days. They wore dresses or they wore skirts with sweaters or blouses. They often wore nylon stockings, hitched to a garter belt, with flats (dainty flat shoes); the alternative was crew or knee socks with shoes. Skirt or dress lengths had to fall at the knee, and given that this was the age of the mini-skirt, this was an interesting rule to enforce. The school did not allow beehive or duck-tail haircuts and students couldn't wear hats in school.

For the teachers, the men had to wear a suit—or dress pants and a sports coat—and always a tie. Women had to dress conservatively and professionally and similarly to the young girls. They wore proper shoes and skirts or dresses and they could not wear pants. There wasn't yet any such thing as a pant suit, so that wasn't even an issue. There were strict dress codes for everyone, but there was nothing wrong with junior-high girls wearing purple knee socks.

The girls looked rather bonny with their like-color, violet socks and it looked like they had a great camaraderie with one another. I was often asking myself questions: Is this a club? Is it a sports team? Is it a musical troupe? Is it a fund-raising gimmick? Is it part of the Girl Scouts? Is it just a fashion statement? However, I didn't think it was important enough to ask anyone else, including the girls. Besides, junior-high girls love to dress identically and sometimes they get pretty silly about it.

It eventually became clear what it was and that it was none of the above. It was a co-ed organization which the school did not recognize or sanction. Yes, boys belonged, but they didn't wear any particular clothing that would identify them as members. The girls were the messengers in the association and the knee socks were the message. If the girls wore purple knee socks on Thursday, it meant they were ready to have sex that afternoon. The boys and girls knew to meet in the courtyard after school. And they did. ... Twelve- and thirteen-year-old boys and girls gathered, moved to a pre-determined place, and had sex. It might be at someone's empty house or it might be at the back of the school. Wherever it was, it was the Milltown-Junior-High-School-Student-Sex-Club. Eventually someone figured it all out. It was probably Ms. Over-Zealous, the teacher who had towed me to the principal's office. She was a one-woman, one-person, SWAT squad.

I *was* shocked. I *was* naive. Are you kidding me? *Are you kidding me*? Twelve- and thirteen-year-olds? I don't know about student growth and development, but there was definitely social and *other* interaction involved. These twelve- and thirteen-year-olds weren't working in the mills.

# Chapter 3

## Trouble in Paradise

"Señorita Christen," Joel asked, "how do you say 'football team?'"

"Teama de Futbal."

"Señorita Christen," Mindy wondered, "how do you say 'makeup?'"

"Maikio"

"Señorita Christen, how do you say 'I love my boyfriend?'" Julie wanted to know.

"Amo mi chico amigo."

I couldn't speak Spanish; I couldn't understand Spanish; I didn't know how to use the language lab. But there I was teaching beginning and intermediate Spanish, sometimes even making up words so I didn't have to say, "I don't know." Mostly I was learning right along with the students. In my second year, I was so ingenious as to divide one class with multiple levels of learning ability into three parts and teach them simultaneously at those different levels. That meant different homework, different classwork, and keeping two-thirds of the class busy while I was working with the other third. No trivial feat. And this was only one of my five classes.

All went reasonably well, notwithstanding the colossal amount of planning I had given myself. There was one student, however, who got under my skin. There I was trying to balance teaching beginning Spanish to thirty-five students in three different groups and if it hadn't have been for Kevin, I would have thought the whole thing a victory.

He mocked me. He dissed me. He made faces behind my back. He did things with his fingers. He aggravated me. He infuriated me. He owned his self-designated role of disrupting the class and took that job and responsibility seriously. I guess someone had to do it. I tried all the common approaches—talking quietly to him; impressing on him the need for paying attention; explaining the importance  of consideration for others; keeping him after class; and, of course, when I had reached my limit of tolerance, angrily commanding, "Kevin, go to the office ... *now*!" Kevin was nothing if not persistent and relentless. Out of ideas and approaches, one day when I kept Kevin after school, in a fiercely furious tone I barked, "Kevin, just stand there and don't move." And he did. He stood on a square tile in front of my desk for an hour. I know; I know. I was at my wit's end. I hadn't just lost my wits; I hadn't just lost my patience; I had lost my mind.

There is much research that shows that starting at around age ten, young people are beginning to learn, and to practice, new and more abstract and advanced ways of thinking, and it's true that provoking adults and engaging them in verbal duels and then gleefully watching what happens is just one way of fine tuning their new cognitive skills. Kevin was definitely into fine tuning.

But, Kevin and Spanish weren't my only issues. American geography turned out to be an unexpected minefield. The school provided geography books with a publication date of 1909. This was 1963 and 1964. The books were tattered, ripped, missing pages, and completely out-of-date in both content and design. I had a brilliant idea. Have the students buy Steinbeck's *Travels with Charley*, just recently published in 1962, and learn cultural and physical geography through Steinbeck's cross-country trip. We would create our own maps and discuss different ways of life in our country as we journeyed along with Steinbeck and his French *bleu* poodle,

Charley, otherwise known as *Charles le Chien*. I didn't know that public-school teachers couldn't ask students to buy books. Too late; it was already done. I received my first office-invitational to visit with the principal over that. Surprisingly, all the students did get the books, but I didn't anticipate the coming explosion.

The problem started brewing already around page twenty. Steinbeck and Charley, heading up to Maine, were on a ferry going from Long Island to Connecticut when Steinbeck got in a conversation with a fellow passenger who was stationed on a submarine in New London. The sailor was on leave but happy to discuss submarines, some of which were in the water nearby and on which several of his family members had served. The sailor described his own experience:

> *Nice thing about it is if there's a storm, you can submerge, and it's quiet. Sleep like a baby and all hell busting loose up above.*

And several pages later in the book, after attending a church service in Vermont, Steinbeck commented,

> *But this Vermont God cared enough about me to go to a lot of trouble kicking the hell out of me.*

And then as Steinbeck was thanking a man for directions somewhere around Niagara Falls, the man replied,

> *Hell, ... I ain't even got you out of town yet.*

At a lake outside of Gary, Indiana, as Steinbeck parked his trusty and beloved Rocinante, his specially built truck-home named for Don Quixote's horse, a security guard jumped out of a jeep proclaiming the land to be private property. But Steinbeck invited him into his truck-home for coffee and the young man grinned and responded,

> *What the hell, you don't build no fires and you don't throw out no trash.*

Have you figured out the problem? Or are you as oblivious as I was?

My second office-invitational: *Meet with Mr. Hawn on Friday at 2:30 p.m.* I did, and I got an earful and reprimand about my lack of judgment regarding student reading material.

"Marilyn, why would you assign a book with the word *hell* in it? Didn't you know parents would be furious?" Mr. Hawn asked.

"I didn't really notice it; I guess I was only paying attention to the geography," I replied.

"Did you read the book yourself?" he quizzed.

"Yes, of course," I fired back quickly. I hadn't, but that seemed like the right response. Internally, I tried to shift the blame to the parents as I asked myself, "What high-school parents read their teenagers' books, anyway?" My ingenious idea wasn't so ingenious after all.

And the parents and the principal didn't even know what was down the road in the book. Neither did I. What would have happened if we had continued reading the book? On went Steinbeck and Charley. After traipsing past that lake in Gary, Indiana, and into Chicago, there was Steinbeck at the Ambassador East Hotel, exhausted, and waiting for his wife to join him from NY. He had convinced the management to let him use a room not yet cleaned to just freshen up. And in that room, Steinbeck re-created in his mind, and described in the book, what must have happened in the room the night before. It wasn't pretty. That wouldn't have been good for students to read.

On the other hand, what would have come later in the book would have been a terrific cultural-geography escapade. Onward Steinbeck went in his three-quarter-ton pickup to the Twin Cities, to Fargo, the Bad Lands, Billings, Yellowstone,

Idaho, Spokane, and Seattle; through the redwoods of Oregon, down to San Francisco, over to the Mojave Desert; and back east into Arizona, New Mexico, Texas, and finally into New Orleans. The South was deep in racial conflict, and things were very tense as issues got heated over voting rights; privileges, or lack thereof, on buses, in bathrooms, and at lunch counters; school desegregation; and employment discrimination—the very issues to which Dr. Martin Luther King Jr. had spoken on The National Mall. Steinbeck's descriptions of the spreading and heightening racial fire in the South, including, as he saw it, the common use of the word *nigger*, would have inspired some unpredictable classroom discussions.

There was the day Steinbeck drove into a parking lot on the edge of New Orleans. The parking-lot attendant approached his window and said,

> *Man, oh man, I thought you had a nigger in there. Man, oh man, it's a dog. I see that big old black face and I think it's a big old nigger.*

Once Steinbeck assured him it was a dog and not a *nigger,* the attendant let him park and got him a cab. The taxi driver asked Steinbeck where he was from. When Steinbeck cleverly told him that he was from Liverpool, to avoid all conflict in the racially-charged atmosphere, the driver responded,

> *Well, you'll be all right. It's the goddamn New York Jews cause all the trouble.*

Steinbeck took the bait and asked what he meant.

> *Why, hell, mister. We know how to take care of this. Everybody's happy and getting along fine. Why, I like niggers. And them goddamn New York Jews come in and stir the niggers up. They just stay in New York there wouldn't be no trouble.*

*Hell, Jews, goddamn, and niggers.* This would have been the quadfecta of my firing.

None of this happened. After the office reprimand, we abandoned the book and regressed to the utterly boring, 1909, moldy version of American geography. I had learned my lesson about parental power and consequences of actions. I would never give an assignment again without previewing it. I mean never, ever.

# Chapter 4

## Petitions, Persistence, and Protests

There was yet another troublesome event that second year. A group of teachers started a petition pledging that male teachers would *not* have to wear suit jackets, sports coats, or ties on days when the temperature reached ninety degrees. This was the Northeast. There was no air conditioning in these schools. It also stated—*hallelujah!*—that only teachers with five or more years of experience would supervise the cafeteria study hall and they would rotate that duty monthly. It took me not a nanosecond to sign that petition.

A week later a kind of manifesto came around to all the classrooms. This one was from the superintendent of schools, Mr. Chauncy:

> *For all of those who signed the petition regarding men's clothing and the cafeteria study hall, please sign this form to have your name removed.*

Sign a form to remove my name? He wanted us to take our names off the original petition? I saw *red*! Already the superintendent had required me to accept an agreement in my hiring contract that I would not get married while teaching at this school. That was not an atypical requisite for single, female teachers in 1963, but that didn't make it any less of an affront to me and my sense of personal liberty. Congress had not yet passed the Civil Rights Act, which would forbid hiring discrimination on the basis of race, ethnicity, religion, or sex. And even if Milltown had hired me after passage of the law, it might not have mattered. Passing the Civil Rights Act was one thing, enforcing it was another.

Even with the dearth of teachers, I had had to capitulate on that hiring contract to get the job, but I wasn't relenting on this petition. Two weeks later, after the superintendent's decree had made the rounds, minus my signature, I found my third office-invitational: *Meet with Superintendent Chauncey on Tuesday, April 5 at 2:30 p.m.* I sheepishly crawled to that meeting and knew from the beginning what was going to happen. Milltown High School would drop me unceremoniously at the end of the school year.

There are two things you should know in thinking about this. First, remember Kevin, my nemesis? He was Mr. Chauncey's son. I knew that from the first day Kevin walked into my class. I had made a purposeful effort not to give him preferential treatment. Maybe that was a mistake. Maybe I had gone too far in the other direction.

The second thing you should know is that my best friend at Milltown was a former high-school friend, Joan Carlson, who was an English teacher in the high school. She also happened to be one of the school's representatives to Milltown's chapter of the Massachusetts Teachers Association. Massachusetts didn't have unions at that time. What they did have, this association, was a relatively loosey-goosey organization with very little power.

Regardless, it was all we had and I asked Joan to speak to the superintendent on my behalf; at the very least, I wanted to know the exact reasons for my dismissal. Abandoning a study hall routinely; or forcing a student, who happened to be the superintendent's son, to stand for an hour on a foot-square tile in detention; making up words in Spanish; or assigning a questionable book—those might be reasons for dismissal. Refusing to remove my name from a petition? I don't think so. The official reasons:

*Reason #1: Ms. Christen did not show consistency in*

*putting pegs under the fire doors connecting the junior-high building with the high-school building.*

*Reason #2: Ms. Christen was not consistent in raising her window shades on cloudy days.*

Guilty as charged.

The only people who knew about the study hall, the Spanish neologisms, and the detention fiascos were I, the Spanish classes, the study hall students, and Kevin. Apparently none of the students had been talking. And maybe the *Travels with Charley* debacle hadn't been as bad as I had thought.

You don't really think my dismissal had anything to do with doors and window shades, do you? Maybe with not signing the superintendent's manifesto? Maybe?

A few days following Joan's meeting with the superintendent, and after the students had discovered the news about my upcoming discharge, I was preparing to leave the building at the end of classes when I heard a loud roaring noise coming from the front of the school. I scrambled to another room so that I could see what the hullabaloo was. I was dumbfounded when I looked out the window and saw what appeared to be the entire student body—including Kevin, yes, including Kevin—in front of the school carrying big signs and loudly protesting my expulsion.

"Save Ms. Christen; save Ms. Christen; save Ms. Christen; we want Ms. Christen," they were chanting, over and over.

This was the early 1960s after all. These students had been living with news of protests, sit-ins, marches, and all kinds of civil-rights clashes in the country. It was the era. During the previous week, Dr. Martin Luther King, Jr., after leading two bloody marches that month, had led his third; it was the thousands-strong-voting-rights march from Selma to Montgomery, and we had discussed it in the history and geography classes.

My history students knew about the four black men, Joseph McNeil, Franklin McCain, David Richmond, and Ezell Blair Jr., from the North Carolina Agricultural and Technical College. On February 1, 1960, they had walked into Woolworth's in Greensboro, NC; they had bought some college supplies and then had gone to the lunch counter and had waited to be served. It was a segregated lunch counter, so no one served them. They sat there until the store closed. My students knew that although this sit-in wasn't successful, subsequent sit-ins were. Black college students sat-in at Woolworth's and S.H. Kress stores in several cities in the next two weeks and by 1961, over seventy thousand had participated in sit-ins. It was these sit-ins and protests that had led to the section in the Civil Rights Act of 1964 that declared segregation at lunch counters unlawful.

My classes also knew about Grandma Beckford. In 1940, being way ahead of her time, she ran for the City Legislature in Ward Seven in Worcester, MA. She didn't win the election, but she never let that defeat or being a woman or being a young widow stop her from doing anything. When she wanted something done for her city or her district or her neighborhood, she went to City Hall and sat there until someone acknowledged her and her cause.

There was the bus problem. Grandma Beckford lived at the top of a very steep hill and whatever bus she and those who lived on the hill took, they had to get off at the bottom and walk the three-quarters of a mile up that arduous, and, in the dark, scary Heard-Street incline. So, Grandma Beckford—who could be rough, tough, and, sometimes, gruff—went to City Hall and sat-in for three days and nights until, finally, the city agreed to change the routes and send buses up the Heard Street hill. She was the original sitter-in, I think.

Republicans!!

# Anna H. Beckford

Is Anxious To Serve
Ward Seven

AS ITS

# Representative

In The Legislature

She Solicits Your Support at the
PRIMARIES, TUESDAY, SEPTEMBER 17, 1940

Regardless of when the first sit-in was, yes, these students at Milltown High knew how to do it. A few weeks earlier they had staged a sit-in in the cafeteria over the bad food, and who could blame them. They also knew how to organize and carry out a protest and they knew how to march. And so they did on my behalf. This was remarkable; this was awesome; this was so the 1960s. Thank you, students. Well done. Way to *make* history. I guess I had done something right in my classes.

Maybe it was the support of the Teachers Association; maybe it was the student protest; or maybe it was the newly signed Civil Rights Act which, besides forbidding discrimination in hiring, provided for equal treatment for women in the work place. Whatever it was, the superintendent reversed himself and offered me a new contract. I promptly declined.

In June, 1965, almost a year after the Civil Rights Act became law, I walked down the front steps of Milltown Junior-Senior High School for the last time. There in my rear-view mirror were my Spanish-teaching days. I would never again make up words in Spanish ... unless, of course, it was absolutely necessary.

.

# PART II

## *THE MIDDLE*

## Chapter 5

## Teaching on Foreign Land, Allan, and a Headache

It wasn't really foreign land, but it was definitely foreign to me. After a year in graduate school, where I tried to ramp up my sorely limited command and arsenal of world and U.S. history, I found a teaching position in a northern city of Indiana. It wasn't a nice city. Let's just say we all called it *Sin City*. This seemed made for me—a low-income, rather dingy, neglected city whose police department had just arrested a man posing as a policeman, stopping women at red lights, jumping in their cars, demanding they drive somewhere, and then raping them. I wasn't looking for that, but the city and the high school oozed disadvantaged. They were ripe for rescuing, by me, of course. I was still thinking it was my job to save the world.

Glenridge High School was a very large high school, much larger than Milltown. That first week of school, September, 1966, the administration summoned me and other new teachers to go to the paddle room for instructions in paddling. Paddling? What is paddling? What is a paddling room? And the next thing I knew, there we were in a room that looked like a large, empty closet—no windows, nothing really in the room at all. The principal handed each of us a foot-long wooden paddle. *Our very own paddles*. The directions:

> *have the student bend over and touch his toes;
> *have a witness—either another student (and what could be a better learning experience than for a student to witness the humiliation of a fellow student?) or another teacher;
> *swat the student on his behind three times.

"Now, let's practice a couple of times with each other."

"Practice?" "Where am I?" "*Practice?*" My brain kept loop-ing over and over. Help! I couldn't shut it off. I never did use a paddle.

That's not to say that there weren't students who brought me close to the edge, but problems at Glenridge High School in all of my classes—all U.S. history and all  full of seniors—were mostly associated with the students falling asleep in class. Many of them worked the 3 p.m. to 11 p.m. shift at the steel mills. This was, after all, not only *Sin City*, it was also *Steel City*. The students came into school half dead and it didn't get any better during the school day.

And there were the black-leather jackets that seemed, at first, so innocuous. Every young man, and many of the young women, in Glenridge High wore a black-leather jacket. Own-ing a black-leather jacket wasn't the problem.  But the school policy prohibited students from wearing their coats to their classes.  Students ignored the rule because they knew that any clothing in a locker would be stolen clothing.

Additionally, and yet again, an administration thought I was the perfect person to manage a multi-person study hall, by myself.  This study hall was not in the cafeteria, it really *was* in a hall, a corridor.  The desks were four deep and there were two hundred students in fifty rows. Maybe I exaggerate. Maybe it was only one hundred students in twenty-five rows. It seemed like twelve hundred students and three hundred rows.  No one was collapsing tables; no one was pitching pens; no one was dropping pennies; no one was even chatter-ing.  Mostly they were sleeping at their desks.  The problem? They all had their security-blanket, black-leather jackets with them and I was supposed to enforce that rule that no one could wear a jacket in school.  As the students warmed up, most of the jackets ended up on the floor and sometimes made the hallway almost impassable. I ignored these two hundred leather jackets (or one hundred or twelve hundred) for awhile. But after many warnings to this lethargic mob, I just grabbed all the jackets, put them in a whopping pile, and asked several students to take them in bunches to the office.

My fourth office-invitational: *See me today. NR.*

The principal was extremely annoyed with the disruption I had caused in his office, and being a very insightful man, he recognized my incompetence and promptly moved me to a study room with ten students in it. Now why hadn't they assigned me that study room in the first place?

School wasn't my only challenge. I was living on the South Side of Chicago on the *wrong side of the Midway* as Chicagoans would say. I was getting used to crime. I lived in the neighborhood of the fifteen hundred or so Blackstone Rangers, a well-organized, well-disciplined, scary, terrorist, street gang that seemed suddenly to crop up in the summer of 1966, as if the Wicked Witch of the South Side said, "Poof," and there they were.

They were young and threatening; the twenty-two-year-old leaders were the oldest members of the gang. Within an hour, they could activate a thousand or more troops for whatever the reason. Maybe it was to picket (everyone picketed in the 1960s), or maybe it was to kill. Besides committing about twenty-five shootings a month, they forced businesses and little kids to pay them dues which they then used to post bail for members who were in jail. In juxtaposition to that brutality and bullying, they were social Robin Hoods who fought for improvements in their neighborhood and demonstrated in front of City Hall on behalf of their tribe. They headquartered and met regularly in the Presbyterian Church.

I never personally witnessed them committing a crime.

Everyone in the neighborhood had a telephone number to call to make the required contact on entering or exiting the area and as long as we followed their rules, we were safe and they protected us. They knew who we were and where we lived because when we had moved in, we had had to register with them. But, one day a stray bullet came through the living-room window of our brick townhouse opposite the University of Chicago Law School. Our response—we were four women—was to get an over-sized, blow-up-male-rubber-doll from Neiman Marcus, name him Rubber Man, and sit him in the living-room chair so any creep or thief looking in our window would think there was a big, strong man in the house.

It was because of the bullet that, shortly afterwards, when a four-year-old, very tiny, neighborhood salesperson, holding a cute little German Shepherd puppy, knocked on our door, we said, "Yes, we want to buy your puppy." The puppy, named Hercules, and Rubberman would keep us safe. Although we went to bed that night feeling much safer, that sense of security didn't last long. The next day, Hercules was missing. It didn't take much time to figure out that the four-year-old and his cohorts were selling and stealing and re-selling and re-stealing the same puppy over and over. Entrepreneurship begins early in the *hood*, especially when the young businessmen have to pay dues to their overlords.

Compared to living in this fast paced, dynamic neighborhood, where the teens were into killing, extortion, and a heavy social agenda, it seemed rather tame that day, when I drove into the parking lot at Glenridge High School, an hour away, and saw something dangling on the school's back doors. As I got closer, I realized there were dead chickens decorating all four entrances. What they symbolized I have no idea. It was probably some students' idea of a fun thing to do. And at the end of that same day, I exited the building to find the chickens and my car's radio antenna gone. My beautiful, red, Volkswagen beetle, along with many other cars, had been spray-painted a lovely black and white in various and clever geometric patterns. Glenridge teens were into chickens and art.

And also into fighting. We were never to get involved in student fights. Our instructions were, "Call the office on the intercom and the office will call the police." There were no phones in classrooms in those days; there was just the intercom to the office, and some rooms didn't even have that. And so there was the day when there was a gigantic food fight in the cafeteria. I had never witnessed a food brawl before. As a way of explanation, while Sin City was largely a minority city, the population of this particular high school was mostly white. But a couple of busloads of black students arrived daily to join the student body. It was a monumental clash that day between these bused students and the local students.

While it is messy, flying food is infinitely and always better than flying bullets. The administration called the police and the melee eventually came to an end with no serious physical injuries. It was kind of funny. The kids were wearing pasta and sauce. The pasta was hanging down their faces and looked like strings of red hair. Almost everything on the day's menu decorated the cafeteria walls and floor, and the police, and especially their hats, were bejeweled in the same pasta and sauce and also in chocolate pudding that the students seemed to have reserved just for them. One of the policemen had a blob of the pudding right over his eyes. All the tables lay upside down in the mess on the floor. What is it about high school students and cafeteria tables?

My teaching in Glenridge High School was spectacularly

unspectacular. How long was it going to take me to know what I was doing? This was my first time teaching U.S. history and it was a mediocre experience at best. It was already a problem that I had never found U.S. history very interesting. To add to that, the U.S. history curriculum in public schools is, and for over one hundred years has been, very disjointed. Typically, it is split into two halves—pre-1865 history in the eighth grade and post-1865 history in the eleventh or twelfth grade. What cockeyed excuse was there for this system? What looney national or local committee thought it was a good idea to put three or four years between one part of the history and the other? Was it the usual territorial demands of teachers at different grade levels that had led to this pattern or had it just continued this way because of those demands?

Trying to teach post-1865 U.S. history to narcoleptic seniors who hadn't remembered a single thing from the eighth grade about pre-1865 U.S. history presented a challenge I didn't quite meet. You can't expect students, least of all sluggish ones, to make sense of the Reconstruction after the Civil War without remembering the Civil War and you can't expect them to understand the Civil War without knowing what led up to it. I had to review the entire pre-1865 history before I could even begin. Ripping out all my fingernails would have been an easier and less painful task.

"Nope, I don't remember," Rob claimed.

"I never heard of that," Seth contended.

"I don't think we learned about that," said Mary.

"We never had that," Carla added.

And on and on went the excuses. They could hardly lift their heads off their desks. Put these two factors together— exhausted students and an indifferent, unexcited teacher. That is a recipe for one of two things: student misbehavior of monumental proportions or student apathy and lethargy. It is not a recipe for learning. I felt like I was napping on my feet five periods a day, and they *were* napping. I could hardly creep through the day. I had had moments of creative brilliance in my teaching at Milltown, but I hadn't really figured out the whole teaching thing. There was nothing creative going on in my classes at Glenridge. Teaching hadn't been in my plans, remember.

While I was working in Sin City, my dear high-school friend Allan was serving our country in Vietnam. His dream had been to complete his graduate work at American University and become a diplomat, but he had put that vision on hold when the Vietnam War began. We were all learning, if we didn't already know it, that fighting was not new to Vietnam. Ho Chi Minh, a thirty-year Vietnamese expatriate, had returned from China during the chaos of World War II intent on freeing Vietnam from sixty years of French control. After his communist Viet Minh forces succeeded in driving out the French in 1954, the Geneva Accords had set up a temporary division of Vietnam at the 17th parallel which put communist North Vietnam north of the line and non-communist South Vietnam south of the line.

But there were Communists, the Viet Cong, in South Vietnam as well. They were waging guerilla warfare against the South Vietnamese, and just before the students at Milltown High had protested my dismissal in 1965, the first U.S. ground troops had arrived in Vietnam to bolster South Vietnam's defenses and to respond to the North Vietnamese firing on two U.S. ships in the international waters of the Gulf of Tonkin, a few months prior.

Allan became a navy pilot, and at about the same time that I began my teaching at Glenridge, he was stationed on the USS

Kitty Hawk, Fighter Squadron 213. On the night of February 4, 1967, while I was still pondering the difference between my violent and philanthropic, dual-purpose, neighborhood teens and those family-oriented, steel-working, chicken-killing, car-painting adolescents at Glenridge High School; and while I was trying to cope with comatose and slumbering students with black-leather jackets; and while my brain was still sorting out the teaching and learning thing, Allan (Lieutenant Allan P. Collamore Jr.), working as the radar intercept officer, and his pilot, Lieutenant Donald E. Thompson, launched their F-4B Phantom fighter aircraft—considered one of the hottest and most maneuverable planes around—on an armed reconnaissance along the coast of North Vietnam.

The two men were wingmen on a two-plane mission. They were supposed to fly in a six to seven mile radar trail behind the flight leader. But a minute after the leader dropped a flare to light up an enemy truck convoy below, he saw a ferocious explosion behind him. He circled back but was unable to make contact with Allan or his pilot. He could only see a large fire below. Search and rescue efforts found nothing and stopped because of enemy fire and darkness; the next day, there were no clues as to what had happened to Allan, his pilot, or their plane.

My Glenridge experience came to an end in June of that year (1967) because the teacher whom I had replaced decided to return from her leave. I was very sad when I left Glenridge. I hadn't had time to save one student, let alone the city;

31

I hadn't succeeded much in awakening and engaging the chronically sleepy students; and I didn't know what had happened to Allan. Although, emotionally, I didn't know how to sort out Allan's disappearance, what I did know was that the war in Vietnam was not just something in a book or on the TV news anymore. I knew that teaching about Vietnam would never be the same again and that it would be different from anything else I taught. It had become personal. I thought it was a really brief headache I had the day I realized this; I know now it was the brain brewery rumbling.

## Chapter 6

## Boston, Tanneries, The Civil Rights Act, and Pigeons

In the midst of that new and unique brain activity, as I had done in Arizona, I headed back East to familiar people and places. This was a much more pleasant trip than that awful, cross-country bus ride had been four years before. No bus, no cigars, just an uneventful, fourteen-hour drive filled with thoughts and questions of what I was going to, and what I could, do next.

I didn't have any concrete plan in mind, but ended up living dirt-cheap in the then-brand-new, and the now-exclusive, Prudential Center Apartments right next to Copley Square in Boston (the scene, forty-six years later, of the unthinkable Boston Marathon bombing). The management of the development wanted to fill the buildings quickly and half-price rent sounded pretty good to me. Little did I know that the hotel next door, and several others on Boylston Street in the same vicinity, were, at the time, more brothels than hotels. It would be a whole new adventure in a lively, prostitute-, homeless-, and drug-filled community.

And what better way to immerse myself into my new village than to work, at least for the summer, the 3 p.m. to 11 p.m. shift at the Sun Market which was attached to my apartment building. There I watched and served and met my neighbors—the well-off, stylish, and sophisticated business people, living in the Prudential Center, who were always in a rush and had cursory greetings at best; the colorful, amazingly-dressed, brightly-finger-nail-painted prostitutes and the stripe- and big-lapel-suited, and also brightly-finger-nail-painted pimps who always had plenty of money and who

33

were working the hotels in the area; the *nons-compos-mentis*, long-haired drug addicts who hung out near the Back Bay (train) Station; and the bedraggled, dirty, smelly homeless who came in looking for handouts and to get out of the cold, and who dropped and slept outside the market—wrapped in whatever they could find on the sidewalk—wherever it seemed safe and windless.

While I was learning what *mixed-use district* meant and how much fun it could be living in one, some families in Woburn, a suburb of Boston and a working-class town of about thirty-six thousand, were experiencing something quite different. It had to do with the water.

As far back as the Civil War, Woburn had been home to as many as twenty tanneries; but now only the J.J. Riley Tannery, a subsidiary of Beatrice Food, remained. Leather making had moved to Europe. Other manufacturing, industrial, and chemical companies had moved in. This included the Cryovan Division of W.R. Grace, which manufactured equipment for the food-packing industry and which used solvents for cleaning and for diluting paint and grease; and Unifirst, a uniform and industrial dry-cleaning company.

In 1965, Anne and Charlie Anderson had bought a modest house in Woburn's Pine Street neighborhood, a perfect and quiet place—unlike my environs in Boston—where they could raise children surrounded by nature. A year before, the year of the first Civil Rights Act and the year I had had to abandon *Travels with Charley* in Milltown High School, the town of Woburn had drilled a new well, called well G, in response to the growing population and the need for more water.

The Andersons and others in the neighborhood complained about the taste and smell of the water from the new well. Their complaints seemed to fall on deaf ears and went unresolved. In 1967, the town drilled a second new well, well H. Not only did the water from this well also taste and smell awful, house pipes began to corrode, new appliances were falling apart, and laundry came out of the washing machine covered with stains. That year, there was enough of an outcry that the Massachusetts Department of Health contemplated shutting down both wells. But the town government protested and was allowed to keep the wells open as long as they added more chlorine. The residents, especially Anne Anderson, didn't give up. Their gripes and their voices got louder.

Meanwhile I was counting my blessings that several new and recent pieces of federal legislation put me, a female, front and center as the number one candidate for a position at Woburn High School. Backtracking a little, let me tell you about United States Representative Howard Smith, a Democrat from Virginia, an avid segregationist, and, allegedly, a fool. The story is that he did not want the 1964 Civil Rights Act passed at all; his political position in the South was on the line given that his white, southern constituents liked things the way they were.

As a way to slow down the passage of the Civil Rights Act, at the very last minute Representative Smith had added the word *sex,* in an amendment, to the other constructs—race, color, religion, and national origin—against which you would not be able to discriminate in employment. Allegedly, he thought that the men in the Legislature would not support women's rights and that this addition to the bill would, in effect, kill it. He denied this, but he caused quite a ruckus in the House of Representatives and got the laughs and guffaws he seemingly was hoping for from many of the other men. There were hours of humorous, anti-female debate in the House which got even more riotous after Smith introduced a letter from a female voter who wanted Smith to add another amendment that would fix the imbalance, in the country, of almost two million fewer males than females, so that every female could have a husband.

Well, really, the letter may have been a laughing matter, but discrimination was not. While the men may have thought the whole thing an exercise in hilarity, Martha Griffiths, Representative (D) from Michigan, saw her opportunity and propelled the amendment through the House under Title VII of the Civil Rights Act; Margaret Chase Smith, Senator (R) from Maine, let no dust gather, ran with it, and pushed it through the Senate. Thank you, Representative Howard Smith for introducing the amendment, even if it was for duplicitous reasons and even if, in the end, you voted against the bill.

While the Civil Rights Act was a tremendous step forward for many people, the powers to execute it were weak. Two things happened to add pressure to the enforcement of the Act for women. In 1966, Betty Friedan, a women's rights activist, founded the National Organization for Women (NOW), the partial purpose of which was to make sure there was not gender discrimination in employment. And President Johnson, in 1965 and 1967, expanded President Kennedy's Affirmative Action Order of 1961, so that, in addition to government contractors, any institution receiving federal money had to prohibit employment discrimination and had to promote equal opportunity for women and minorities.

There I was in 1967 applying for the social-studies position in Woburn High School and reaping the benefit of all this legislation and activism. With the combination of the Civil Rights Act, Affirmative Action Orders, and Betty Friedan's NOW, schools became ultimately aware of who they were hiring and how it would impact legal issues and federal money and support. I was in the right place at the right time. Thanks go to all the people who worked for civil rights, including Dr. Martin Luther King Jr., who led the marches; the four black men who sat-in at the Woolworth's in Greensboro, NC; and Betty Friedan, Margaret Chase Smith, and Martha Griffiths who worked tirelessly to gain and enforce civil rights for women and minorities. And thanks, of course, to Grandma Beckford, who fought for her neighbors, her district, and her city; always plowed forward; wouldn't take no for an answer; and taught me that women can do anything. Each of them and many other extraordinary, behind-the-scenes people played a role in my getting the job at Woburn High School in 1967. That and the fact that I was the only female applicant. Thanks to Affirmative Action, Woburn High School would be the next stop on this education train.

That was kind of a coup, my being a social-studies teacher. Prior to 1967, it was an anomaly to see women in the social-studies departments of high schools. This was a male-dominated realm, partly because the social-studies dominions were often, and still tend to be, the launching pads for school football coaches, vice principals, and principals. It was like a medieval society only the nobles could join. And only certain kinds of nobles could join. We could call them the *jock nobles* or, if you wish, the *noble jocks*. Not that prior to my job at Milltown, I cared; not that I had ever wanted to be a teacher; not that I had ever had an urge to teach social studies; not that I understood that at Milltown it was a fluke that I was teaching history and geography. But there I was, the only female in the social studies department.

I remember Woburn High School as enormous, with the old building having been built in the early 1900s and the newer building probably in the 1950s. At the time, I remember the administration telling me it was the largest high school in Massachusetts. I loved that high school. The administration was savvy and respectful, the teachers were exceptional and collegial, the programs were forward-looking, and the students were typically well-behaved and engaged. Just as the community of Glenridge had supported and revered their schools and their teachers, so did the community of Woburn, although, given the built-in skepticism of New Englanders, not to quite the same degree. It was all good: my easy reverse commute from Boston, the school, the people, and my moonlighting job at the Sun Market that kept me in touch with *all* my neighbors—the kaleidoscopic, the razzle-dazzle, the psychedelic, the forlorn, and the upscale.

Back at the high school, besides my teaching responsibilities, there were the obligatory extra-classroom duties. Every morning, I had to stand at the entrance to the school with my trusty yardstick and measure the distance from the bottom of young women's knees to the bottom of the their skirts. Some days there was a traffic jam of young women waiting to be measured. Anything more than one inch and the young women either had to go home and change, or, more frequently, they had to unpin their garment hems which they had tacked up as soon as they had gotten on the school buses. When it was a pinning issue, which it usually was, they had to give the pins to me so they couldn't re-offend during the school day. But that didn't really matter; they always carried extra pins.

And ... I had to send any young woman with a beehive hairdo into the girls' room to wait for me to comb out the coif. The students manufactured this extraordinary hair style, which stood sometimes four inches or so above their heads, by holding up a hunk of hair and pulling the comb down through that wad several times until it was heavily matted.

This was called teasing the hair. Combing out a beehive hair clump was a stupendously awesome task. "Ouch!" "Oh!" "Stop!" "Wait!" "You're hurting me!" And out came the beehive and out came hair, lots of hair. There was no other way. The administration didn't tolerate hair that towered so high that it blocked other students' views. What was not to love about the 1960s?

At Woburn High School, it was yet another overcrowding situation. The school had to open the fourth floor of the old building to accommodate everyone. My room had had a previous life as a chemistry lab, so I lived daily with high counters in-between me and the students—counters with gas jets and sinks and faucets. There were so many desks and chairs crammed in that room, that you couldn't really walk up and down the aisles. They were almost against the blackboard on one side and close to touching the old, tall windows and ratty, peeling radiators on the other. There was one day when one whole row of desks and chairs disappeared as did that number of students. It was the day the Fire Department came to inspect conditions in the school. No overcrowding here, thank you very much. What had the administration done with that row of desks and students? I never knew. The next day the desks and students were back.

If you opened the windows when it got really hot in there, pigeons flew in; first one pigeon, then another pigeon, then another. They came with all their relatives. Whole extended families of pigeons flew in there and hung out. Consequently there were a lot of pigeon droppings in the room. It couldn't have been healthy. Besides the pigeon droppings, there was dust. I had an adjoining, kind of very-large-closet area that no one had used since forever. That room was fascinating. Among other antiques in that room was a four-foot-high, copper-covered bust of Abraham Lincoln; it was a bust that proudly wore it's plaque announcing itself as a gift from the class of 1921.

This was an old building and that room held a lot of information about its history—old desks, old books, old photos, old notebooks, old shelves; layers of dust covered them all. I didn't like the dust, but the room was one of my favorite places. It provided a great place for students to take make-up exams, for me to have private conversations with students about their work or their behavior, and for me to hide. Sometimes teachers need to hide. I don't think the administration even knew that room was there. No one had touched or been on that floor in years.

One good thing about being on that fourth floor was that administrators never went up there. It took way too long and was too strenuous an exercise to climb four double flights of stairs. And we, up there, had no communication with the office other than by student courier. Consequently, nobody bothered us. The downside was the distance from the cafeteria. Lunch time was sixteen-minutes long which made for an interesting challenge. In those sixteen minutes, we had to get down those four double flights of stairs, dodge in and out among the crowds of students, get to the cafeteria in the new building, pick up the food, eat the food, and get back up those same four double flights of stairs to welcome the students back to class. So, that not working very well, I and the other teachers on that fourth floor brought our lunches, ate together, and bonded up among the pigeons in our own little world.

# Chapter 7

# The Vietnam War, Student Differences, and the Water

When I first started teaching at Woburn, in 1967, there were half a million American troops in Vietnam. Just a little more than four months later, on January 30, 1968, almost a year after Allan had gone missing, the communist Vietcong in South Vietnam joined with North Vietnamese forces and attacked about one hundred South Vietnamese cities and towns. This was known as the Tet offensive because it began on the celebration of Tet, the Vietnamese New Year. The combination of nightly-TV-news videos of killed and wounded troops, of villagers on fire trying to flee to safety, of napalm bombs burning and sticking to everything and everyone they touched, and then the discovery that an American officer had ordered every person—and they turned out to be elderly people, women, and children—in the village of Mai Lai to be killed to assure there were no enemy hiding there added to the huge swell of discontent in the United States against the war.

While that agitation grew stronger and louder outside my classroom and school, there was trouble inside as well. Lunch time split my fifth period class in half—half the class was pre-lunch, half the class was post-lunch. One day, while I was still attempting the cafeteria run, I returned to the room after eating to find everything upside down—desks knocked over; chairs on their sides; students' books and work all over the floor; some of the students' work cut up; pages missing out of my attendance and planning books; and pens missing from my desk. At almost the same time that I sent a student to notify the office about what had happened, someone spotted a young man walking outside on the fourth-floor ledge. I don't remember who got him off the precipice or how, but I do remember that he had my missing pens in his shirt pocket. The school put him in an ambulance and sent him to the local hospital for evaluation.

It was Michael Drew. He sat right in the front row of my world-history class. He was a sophomore, usually silent, who rarely contributed to the class unless I asked him to do so and who almost never interacted with other students. But he was not a behavior problem and he did work that was acceptable. So what had happened that day that led him to do this to my room? I didn't know then and I don't know now. I was concerned at this point, though, that he was a risk to me and my class. I had a meeting with the principal.

"I don't want Michael back in my room. He's dangerous," I said with force.

"When Michael returns to school, he will be back in your class," the principal replied with equal force. He was a man of few words.

"I can't teach with him in the room," I continued.

"You will have to," Mr. Patton added, "and that is the way it will be."

Exit Mrs. Page (I had gotten remarried). Mrs. Page = 0; Mr. Patton = 1.

As it turned out, it was moot. Two weeks later, the local police arrested Michael in a stolen car; he hadn't just stolen a car, he had driven around town, had entered two houses in the center, and had forced the women inside the houses to undress. Fortunately, he did not physically hurt the women. The last I heard, all those years ago, he was in a youth detention facility and doctors were treating him for juvenile diabetes.

I never saw Michael again, but I learned to pay a whole lot of attention to very *quiet* students.

And there was Kathryn, a class-A, blue-ribbon whiner. Whine, whine, whine. One excuse after another. On Monday, it would be, "I lost my assignments." And then on Thursday, she would claim, "My little brother ripped my homework." On the next Tuesday, she would cry, "My essay got thrown in the trash by accident." "My mother spilled coffee all over my papers," she would bawl on Wednesday. "The dog chewed up my report," came next.

But then came the one that really sent me into orbit, "My house burned down last night; I couldn't do my homework."

Okay, this young lady needed help. I sent her to the counselor pronto. And it didn't take long for Kathryn and the counselor to appear back at my classroom door. Her house really had burned down the night before. Sometimes even students who cry "Wolf!" a lot, may on one occasion really see a wolf.

And, so, I learned to pay a whole lot of attention to the really *noisy* students.

I admit that I worked hard in my accidental career as a teacher. I really wanted students to learn the basic history of the world, but also to think about what and who in history were important and why and how historical events impacted us even in the present. In my favorite class, ancient history, which I discovered I loved and which the students seemed to love, we were learning about Socrates and his teaching methods. At that time in the United States, there was a very loud and antagonistic conversation and debate revolving around the statement, "God is dead," and *Time* magazine on April 8, 1966, had depicted this argument as its cover had barked in big red letters, on a black background, "Is God Dead?"

What a perfect way to show the students how Socrates taught his students, that is, by invoking thinking and analysis through a process of probative, thoughtful, dialectic, and rigorous questioning. I would put "God is dead" on the board in big letters, and through a similar kind of questioning, I would lead the class into scrutinizing the phrase and recognizing different perspectives, just as Socrates might have done in ancient Greece. Another one of my exceptional ideas. If I do say so myself, the class was intensely involved and energized. Then they took turns creating different variations of the Socratic method using many different topics. Well done, students.

Two days later, my fifth office-invitational arrived: *Meet with Mr. Patton and Mr. Kelly* (superintendent) *in superintendent's office on Thursday.* I had upgraded to two administrators. The thing about office-invitationals is that the invitors never let the invitees know what the invitation is about. This gives the invitees time to mentally review everything possible they've done in recent memory and to cause themselves catastrophic mental anguish and harm before they even get to the meeting. I had *no* idea why I was going to that appointment. Maybe it was about next year's schedule; maybe it was about being advisor to the History Club; maybe they wanted to congratulate me on being such an innovative teacher or for doing such a great job combing out beehives.

The meeting began with Mr. Kelly speaking. "Mrs. Page, we appreciate the work you do at Woburn High School, but we are concerned about your ancient-history class. We received a disturbing call from a parent who complained that you are teaching that God is dead. A member of the School Committee also received a call. Could you tell us what is going on in your classroom?"

"*Oy vey*! *Oy vey*! *Oy vey*!" I cried in Yiddish to myself. Had I known then what I know now, I would have asked who, specifically, had contacted them with this faulty information, but I didn't. Instead, I spent the next half hour, explaining what I had been doing in my classes and why.

Even though I hadn't asked and they hadn't told me, I knew instantly who the culprit was. It could only be Patricia, a young lady with (this is the nicest way I can say it) limitations. Yes, she had gone home after what I thought had been a dazzling and juiced-up class and had told her parents that I was teaching that God was dead.

And I learned to pay a whole lot of attention to *learning-challenged* students with comprehension problems.

I loved the students at Woburn High School. They knew when to be serious, when to laugh, when and how to raise questions, when to stop fooling around. Or did I teach them all that? I don't recall, but I do know that they weren't always well-coordinated. There I was waiting for the students to come from their previous classes. As required, I was standing at my doorway ready to thwart any wayward occurrence. Jason, who was sixteen- or seventeen-years-old, was carrying a bunch of books as he was about to enter the room. He slipped on something, the books went flying, and both he and I went forward towards each other to catch the books.

What happened next happened in a flash. Instead of grabbing his books, he … latched onto both my breasts. Whoops; y-ew; perfect aim. His face turned beet-red; my face turned redder-beet-red. Together our faces could have lit up the auditorium. Now what? He was so flustered, he sounded like a toddler trying to speak. He had words, but no verbs; I was so discombobulated, I couldn't speak at all. I could hardly look at

Jason after that.

And I learned to pay attention to *clumsy* students.

I think I was learning something important—that teaching wasn't just about teaching; that nothing worked well, not only if you couldn't or didn't control the classroom, but also if you didn't know who your students were. Was I on the cusp of grasping the hang of it all? I didn't want to leave Woburn High School, just when I seemed to be getting started, just when my feet seemed to be on firmer ground. But in June of 1969, I didn't have any choice. I was pregnant; and the policy in Massachusetts, and many other states at that time, required women to leave work when they were two months pregnant. Schools saw pregnant women as liabilities. After all, they could fall or trip, hurt themselves, and sue the school. Although women had made some progress with the Civil Rights Act and Affirmative Action Orders, it wasn't until 1978, that the Pregnancy Discrimination Act prohibited employment discrimination on the basis of pregnancy or childbirth. Women still had a way to go in 1969.

We, the pregnant teachers, did the only thing we could do. We hid our pregnancies, bought clothes in ever-increasing sizes, and kept quiet. I was five-months pregnant when the school year ended. One of my colleagues didn't even make it. Her baby arrived a month early, the week before the end of school, and no one had known either one of us was pregnant. It was lucky for us that no one ever came up to that fourth floor.

As I left Woburn High School that year in June, fighting in Vietnam continued. There was still no word about Allan. He was one of the almost five hundred MIA troops at that time in Vietnam. In July, Appollo II landed on the moon. Neil Armstrong proudly proclaimed to the world, "One small step for man; one giant leap for mankind." And several weeks later, my baby boy was born—five years after well G and two years after well H had been drilled. In that same month of October, 1969, Anne Anderson—whose baby Jimmy was fifteen-months-old—and the committee which she had helped form to close down the wells had a victory when the town temporarily did just that. We were all still oblivious to the deadly chemicals underground and the havoc they were wreaking and had already caused among local families. None of us knew about or had ever heard of TCE.

On a much lighter note, about five months after my baby was born, and about nine months after I had left Woburn High School, a four-foot-high, copper-covered bust of Abraham Lincoln, proudly wearing a plaque announcing itself as a gift from the Woburn High School class of 1921, appeared on my front lawn. Honest. Lincoln had found a new home. I loved those teachers on the fourth floor.

## Chapter 8

## Children, Three Wars, and Cerebral Cogitation

No matter how you spin it, having three children in five years wasn't the result of my thinking clearly, or at all. That production left its very own, special, what-the-heck imprint on the 1970s. Somehow, though, through that on-going, lost-in-time fog, a new career path sprang to life. I thought why not mix together a role in education with some of my original, world- and people-saving goal. The resulting mental equation looked like this:

Working in a school + saving people (students) =
guidance counseling.

Pretty simple. That is how my mind was working—simply, that is—when it was working at all; and, miraculously, I did manage to integrate studying for that master's degree into the children-raising, chaotic, pea-soup blur.

Jump ahead to 1979. With a new master's degree in hand and my three children all about to be in school, I was settling into another job search when news from Woburn seemed to be making headlines at breakneck speed. In the Spring of 1978, nine years after I had left Woburn High School, police were investigating one hundred and eighty-four barrels of industrial waste found on a vacant lot just north of wells G and H. The state environmental inspector demanded the wells be tested. However, what they found wasn't the polyurethane resin that was in the barrels. What they discovered was tricheloroethyline (TCE) and tetrachloroethylene (PERC), both industrial solvents. Two days later the town closed the wells indefinitely.

A little more than a year later, on September 10, 1979, another headline jarred me. Charles Ryan, a reporter for the *Woburn Daily Times*, cried out about a new problem in his article, "Lagoon of Arsenic Discovered in North Woburn." A construction crew had found a pit, five-feet-deep and almost an acre in size, full of arsenic, lead, and other heavy metals. Woburn once again had my attention, and long overdue, I did my research and started putting the history of putrid Woburn water and contamination together. I didn't know that Jimmy Anderson had leukemia or that two other children in the same neighborhood, no, the same block, had it also. I didn't know that Anne Anderson had spent the decade since I had left Woburn trying to get someone to listen to her concerns about the horrible water.

There was no end to my lack of knowledge of what had been going on in Woburn. Although there had been enough complaints to get the wells shut down just after I left in 1969, the following spring, while I was taking care of my new baby, the town of Woburn had needed more water and their engineers had ordered the wells open again. And for the next several years, the town had oscillated, opening and closing the wells many times, until that 1978 discovery of the TCE and the PERC contaminants finally closed the wells for the last time.

Once these water contaminants had been found and identified, Rev. Bruce Young, the local Episcopal minister—with whom Anne Anderson had sought solace and help after her three-and-a-half-year-old son Jimmy had been diagnosed with leukemia, in January of 1972—now rallied to her side. No longer thinking she was an hysterical, overreacting mother with a sick child, Rev. Bruce published a letter in the *Woburn Daily Times* inviting town residents who knew anyone who had had leukemia in the last fifteen years to come to a meeting at his church. The results of that meeting, which took place on October 4, 1979, showed that there had been twelve cases of leukemia in Woburn since the opening of wells G and H; eight were located in East Woburn, and a cluster of six was right in the Andersons' Pine-Street neighborhood.

Two months later, on December 12, 1979, the *Woburn Daily Times* bellowed another headline: "Child Leukemia Answers Sought." It was yet another Charles Ryan story; he apparently had become the voice for the Woburn families. Tragically, a little more than a year after the *Times* had published that story, on January 18, 1981, young Jimmy Anderson died of leukemia at age thirteen. Anne Anderson's fight against the town, its industrial businesses, and its ghastly water took on a whole new meaning.

Back at the beginning of the 1970s, shortly after I had left Woburn High School, while Anne Anderson was receiving the awful news that Jimmy had leukemia and while she was fighting her never-ending war trying to get authorities to investigate the connection between the nasty-tasting water and the increasing numbers of seriously sick children, the Vietnam War continued to impact the whole country in one way or another. Troops continued to die; the number of MIA and wounded grew. The nightly Vietnam-War-TV-horror-show continued to enter homes at dinnertime, disturbing families and meals. Never before had there been such a TV bombardment of death, massacre, and gore. Yes, we could have shut it off and ignored the war. It wasn't that easy to do.

Finally, in January of 1973, the Paris Peace Accords agreed to a ceasefire in Vietnam and our troops were on their way home, if only to a muted and sometimes angry reception; jeers, not cheers, met them as they landed in the middle of intense anti-war demonstrations. And, although the war was over and the deadly TV-Vietnam-War-show came to an end, another TV-war-show—court-ordered busing in Boston—replaced it. Now there was a new war right in my own back yard.

The first skirmish of this war had occurred in March, 1972, when fourteen parents and forty-four children brought a class action against the Boston School Committee, the Boston Superintendent of Schools, the Massachusetts Board of Education, and the Massachusetts Commissioner of Education. The suit claimed that the city of Boston purposefully segregated its schools.

Ruling on this class action, in 1974, Federal Judge Arthur B. Garrity found the Boston School Committee had intentionally, through neighborhood districting, brought about and maintained segregated schools in violation of the U.S. Constitution and the 1964 Civil Rights Act. He ordered the city of Boston to bus thousands of black students from one section of the city to another and to send thousands of white students in other directions. And every year the Boston School System was to review the population demographics and change the district lines and busing accordingly.

Bostonians are gritty and scrappy and loyal and sarcastic, all good qualities held dear if you are from Boston. Now, Bostonians in every district were incensed and ostensibly without brains. Neighbor was pitted against neighbor; some parents tried to work with the court order; some tried to thwart the edict. In some families, the wife went one way and the husband the other. Neighborhood schools would no longer be neighborhood schools. The child next door might be going to a different school than your child. The children might have to change schools on a yearly basis.

People roamed the streets at night with metal pipes waiting to smack anyone who didn't belong in their neighborhood or anyone they suspected of supporting the busing. There were informational community meetings and forums that morphed into anti-busing rhetoric, hollering, fighting, and frenzied violence. People hanged and burned effigies of Judge Garrity, Senator Ted Kennedy, and Boston's Mayor White, all busing supporters. Our neighborhoods had become their own war zones, all of it broadcast in full color on the national TV evening news. Boston would reduce itself to a city it didn't recognize.

My five-year-old, the baby who had apparently, in utero, survived the well water of Woburn, would have attended a nice little school up the street but for the busing mandate. Instead, there I was, on September 11, 1974, putting him on a school bus for his first day of school and the first day of forced busing in Boston and then waiting by the TV to see if anti-busing activists or local thugs were stoning, or throwing and smashing themselves against, the buses. The beltings became so frequent and vicious that the school buses needed motor-cycle-police escorts, riot gear and all.

The blatant control center of the anti-busing crusade was the South Boston district of the city. Except for a few blacks scattered here and there, this was a white population—mostly Irish-Catholic families who loved their white neighborhood. They believed busing would change everything, and they were right. The entire junior class of South Boston High School traveled in distaste to Roxbury High School, a school which Judge Garrity had deemed inferior and which was in a predominantly black area. In reverse, Roxbury High School's entire sophomore class took the dreaded buses to South Boston High School where they were met with *GO HOME NIGGERS* spray-painted in bold, grand letters on the street. And that was just the beginning. Buses crisscrossed the city and kids sat on buses sometimes for over an hour, frozen in fear.

And if South Boston was the epicenter of the anti-busing combustion, it was the Bulger brothers, who lived there, who were the obstreperous voices of that upheaval. Brother Bill, a State Senator, verbally railed against the pro-busing, affluent suburbs and the pro-busing politicians and newspaper columnists. He alleged the busing advocates had their own children in private or parochial schools in the city, or in suburban schools, and were not affected. His raised and angry rhetoric spawned more riots. His politically-faithful followers were counting on him to keep South Boston white.

The other brother, the notorious and infamous Whitey Bulger, who twenty years later would be on the FBI's Ten Most Wanted List, and in 2013 would be found guilty of eleven murders and thirty-one counts of racketeering, took a different route. Kevin Cullen and Shelley Murphy, who investigated Whitey Bulger and his roguery for years, allege in their 2013 book—*Whitey Bulger: America's Most Wanted Gangster and the Manhunt that Brought Him to Justice*—that Whitey Bulger's anti-busing activities included chucking a Molotov cocktail into an elementary school in Wellesley and setting the school on fire; anonymously promising to burn down every school in Wellesley (home of Judge Garrity); shooting out all the glass in the front entry of the *Boston Globe* which supported the busing; trying to poison the police horses on guard in South Boston; going to the birthplace home of John F. Kennedy in Brookline, MA and spray-painting *BUS TEDDY* (referring to Ted Kennedy and his support of the busing) on the sidewalk in front of the house; and heaving a Molotov cocktail into the home, setting *it* on fire. No one ever caught or punished him for any of these actions.

With the numerous student and parent boycotts against the busing, especially at the high schools, and the perilous and extended trips to schools that were nowhere near home, little school education occurred that year.  But a whole lot of life learning happened.  As it turned out, the school where the buses took my son was more segregated than his neighborhood school had been pre-busing.  The following year, after the required redistricting, he would be in a different school, and so, on and on it would go, probably a different school every year to meet the imperative of numbers.  It was a horrible and violent time, and we, like many other families, literally gave our home away and moved out of Boston to escape the madness.  We belonged to the *white flight* that in practical terms rendered the experiment and charge a failure in that what had been a mixed-population city with many mixed-population schools became a city of minority schools.

Yes, in September, with his younger brother and sister watching from the front porch, my five-year-old had climbed onto that scary bus for the ride of his life.  That same month, U.S. Intelligence received information concerning an air crash in North Vietnam and the downing of a jet in which two pilots had been killed.  It would be nine months later, as the school year came to an end, and six weeks after South Vietnam officially surrendered to North Vietnam (1975), that the U.S. Government would pronounce Allan and his pilot *presumably killed in action.  Presumably killed in action.  Presumably killed in action.*

But now, as much and as often as I thought about Allan and the Vietnam War, it was not the only thing stuck, and swirling around, in the brain brewery.  While my brain was repeating what it had told me in 1967 when I first learned that Allan was missing—that I would never again teach about Vietnam in a traditional way—now, the brain was shouting loudly, "You will never again teach about industrial contamination or school segregation and desegregation in the same way, either." Brain activity was at an all-time high.

## Chapter 9

## All Kinds of Lesson Designs and No Place to Use Them

Something was happening to me. I was no longer thinking about my own life or local or world events simply as my life, local, or world events. Every time something in life impacted me or people I knew, every time I saw the evening news on TV, and every time I read the headlines or the opinion page or the editorial in the newspaper, my brain kicked into its own strange and free-wheeling gear. It started translating it all into teaching blueprints for me and into all different kinds of learning adventures for adolescents.

Speaking of adolescents, as mystifying as they were most of the time, I think my time at Woburn High School had allowed me a glimmer of understanding of who they were. It wasn't just through the classroom experiences; and it wasn't just by uncovering and paying attention to their individual needs; and it wasn't just because of incidents with Michael or Kathryn or Patricia or Jason. It was also thanks to attending the Friday night football games. Every time I had watched the interplay, teamwork, and camaraderie among the padded-and helmeted-teenage football players, the Tanners; and every time I had seen the same among the black- and orange-uniformed and feathered-hat school band members who played at half-time during those games; and every time I had heard the crazy-cheering-teenage spectators in the stands; and every time one of the kids had said, "Mrs. Page, thanks for coming to the game," the section of the brain brewery reserved for figuring out adolescents would go berserk, almost bubbling over with new awareness of what captured teenagers' attention. As I saw it, that included group or team competition; music; a sense of belonging to, and traveling in, a large peer pack; and support from their teachers.

Given these insights about adolescents and about lesson designs, for at least three topics, my teaching was about to change. The unforgettable wars and personal events of the 1970s—the Vietnam War and what had happened to Allan and thousands like him; Anne Anderson's on-going battle to get something done about the contaminated water and the sick children in Woburn; and the busing conflict in Boston which transformed a whole city into something it wasn't— would not be quiet in my brain. While I searched for a job, the ideas were impatient. Everywhere I went, these thoughts overshadowed everything I did. They were spilling out of my brain the way tears spill out of eyes.

The brain was turning into a machine. A circumstance or experience or new point of view on something, including varying perspectives on teenagers, entered on one side, careened around in and among the other things that were brewing in there and came out on the other side as sparkling would-be history and geography classes. The brain brewery was ablaze. It was almost like an electrified window-shade that kept unrolling and flashing ideas in front of my eyes. Nobody told me, when I carelessly signed onto this career, that my brain would have to be involved and would have to rearrange itself incessantly. Nobody told me ideas would pop into my head any old time and interrupt whatever I was doing. The brain did not  listen when I pleaded, "For crying out loud, leave me alone and let me sleep."

Does this happen to all teachers—all this mental activity? Did all this extemporaneous brain brewing constitute the real teacher training? Did I actually *like* this job?

What could all this brain disarray become? Well, that would be a different book, but as a thimble-full-like preview, for starters, the study of the Vietnam War would become much more hands-on. Students could find Vietnam veterans or their family members—through their town government, by calling the Armed-Services veteran organizations, and by searching their school and town libraries and newspaper archives—and interview them to hear their experiences with, and their slants on, the war.

And we could introduce a *new* topic into the world-history classes—the impact of contaminants on history. For example, by delving into the history of ergot of rye, a fungus that grows on rye and that caused gangrene, convulsions, and death during the Middle Ages, the students would have a whole novel approach to studying the Holy Roman Empire, the Vikings, the history of France, and even witchcraft. (Thankfully, Dad didn't live in the Middle Ages, what with his addiction to rye bread.) And students could figure out the connection among poisoned water, bigotry against Jews, and the Bubonic Plague.

As for the study of mandated busing and civil rights, students could begin by probing the differences between school segregation and desegregation in the South and in the North. What kind of issues and discussions would that induce? What would they discover about themselves through this exercise?

Additionally, it is no small matter that the students would do all of this investigation, inquiry, and examination without computers, which were not yet readily available, and without Google, which was fifteen years in the future. It would be old-fashioned detective work and research that the students would conduct.

Really, is there any program or field in a public school, or any other school for that matter, that couldn't and shouldn't integrate world and life events into its curriculum? The brain brewery—or was it more like a bread pan full of rising dough? —was on fire, all right, but before I could put any of these ideas into action while, at the same time, connecting them to what I had learned about adolescents, and before I lost track of all these shining designs, I had to find a job. It was not all that easy. There was no teacher shortage in the late 1970s as there had been when I had first jumped onto this train. On the contrary, there was a glut of teachers that was about to get bigger.

Talk about bad timing. The voters of Massachusetts passed the Proposition 2½ Initiative in 1980. It would limit municipal tax increases to two and one-half percent each year, and school budgets, funded mainly through local property taxes, would feel this projected deficit severely. School districts were skittish about hiring anyone; actually, they were looking for ways to reduce the budget and they began to lay off everyone they considered superfluous. Guidance counselors would go first. Uh, ha, yes, my well-thought-out plan to drift sideways out of the teaching role and into guidance counseling was, well, ... in tatters. Next to go would be the teachers of the unnecessary—as many would say—electives of art, music, and shop. Those teachers were on the line. Last to go, as always, would be the noble-jock coaches. Would I ever find a job?

## Chapter 10

## Down the Rabbit Hole in Norwalk

It must have been divine intervention of almighty magnitude, or maybe it was because Karma had not yet finished with me over the Sailor-Man crisscross, that I got a job at Norwalk Junior High School. I thought I had learned everything I needed to know about junior-high students back at Milltown. I definitely knew about their fascination with bodily functions. But almost twenty years later, I would discover that I had barely touched the tip of the iceberg. It was frightening. Blindingly, outrageously frightening. Karma had definitely come back for a visit.

What did I learn at Norwalk? You might be sorry you asked.

When you step through the door of a junior-high school—or now, more likely a middle school—nothing is as it seems. You enter an alternate universe. It is sort of like going down Alice's rabbit hole where everything is topsy-turvy. Things in this junior-high-middle-school universe get more and more curious daily. The students, like Alice did in Wonderland, are all asking, "Who in the world am I?" and wondering why they are so different from everyone else. They all go about this identity search in the strangest and most relentlessly different ways, flailing and cavorting about.

For some students in seventh and eighth grades, hormones are firing on all cylinders; for others, there is barely a spark. Some boys have heavy, thick  moustaches and beards, others have hairless, soft, baby-bottom faces. Some of the girls have gigantic, mountain-like breasts, standing out sort of like Mt. Ranier and her sister volcanic mountain, Mt. St. Helens; others are flat-chested, not even buds there. And if girls do have breasts, the junior-high reasoning goes, they must be sluts. Girls can be as mature and as tall as sixteen-year-olds and probably feel like Alice did when she was nine-feet-tall in her *Adventures in Wonderland*; boys can look like they escaped from fourth grade and feel like they are ten-inches-tall as Alice did when she ate cake.

Junior high is not a pretend rabbit hole; it's the real deal. The oddest things happen to these seventh and eighth graders. They lose the ability to walk, even after twelve years of practice. They trip. They trip over their own feet; they trip over random feet; they trip over nothing at all. The most precarious place for a student to be in seventh or eighth grade is in front of an open locker. Just from sheer klutziness, one can and does fall in. If that doesn't happen, a peer cannot pass someone in front of his open locker without accidentally-on-purpose shoving him in and slamming the door. That is why when you walk down a junior-high or middle-school corridor, you hear, "Let me out! Let me out! Let me out!" It isn't your imagination. There are children embedded in their lockers.

Chaperoning a junior-high-school dance is like waiting for the second coming. The girls and boys stand against opposite walls in the gym pretending to hate each other and acknowledging and proclaiming, on one side, that girls are *dumb* and, on the other side, that boys are *so stupid*. It's not nice, but it is what happens. Eventually some brave girl crosses the great divide and asks a boy to dance. The tallest girl always must ask the shortest boy. This is the way of the junior-high world. As in Alice's *Looking Glass House*, things go the wrong way in here.

The dance itself gives new meaning to the words awkward and graceless; the faces of the monster girl and the elfin boy ooze pain and misery. It's hard to link hands with someone when one thinks it's icky to do so. Where does one put one's hands, anyway? What if you step on your partner's feet? In which direction do you go? What if someone laughs at you? What if someone looks at you? What if you fall down? There is so much to think and worry about. And yes, some of these kids in junior high, who find it vexatious and perilous to dance or hold hands, are some of the same students who belong to a purple-knee-sock club.

Once students are at the junior high, one of the most useful things they learn is how to give *flats*. These aren't the same flats that girls and teachers wore to school in the 1960s. Those were pretty shoes with maybe half-inch heels. These *flats* are referring to flat tires. You cause a flat tire by stepping on the back of someone's sneaker. The back of the sneaker collapses, the sneaker gets a flat, and the student falls out of her shoe. What could be more comical? Maybe giving two flats at the same time. That is the way to start your day off right. It's like having triple, hot fudge sauce on your sundae (well, that would be the comparison for me anyway).

It seems as if brains either haven't developed, have developed unevenly and are askew, or go into hibernation in junior high. I think it is that way so that when the students leave this strange anomaly of the junior high and enter the ninth grade, their brains are more coagulated, ready to erupt, and prepared to practice analytically and comprehensively engaging teachers in long-lasting mental combat and scrimmage to cause them whatever stress and angst they can. Once in high school, like carnivorous plants, the brains are ready to inter and devour the teachers in their traps. Until then, these junior-high brains lay in wait, in limbo, for their upcoming, sprouting debuts. Back in Milltown High School, Kevin's brain must have practically burst apart when he entered ninth grade. No wonder he acted the way he did.

The modern-day middle schools typically add fifth and sixth grades to the seventh- and eighth-grade-junior-high configuration. Some people think the middle-school architecture and curriculum came out of, and incorporates, a new and more in-depth philosophy based on the *Turning Points* Carnegie Report of 1989, which addressed the needs of ten- to fourteen-year-olds. Others know for certain that many middle schools came to life because of a combination of student demographics, available district school buildings, the school budget, and the pragmatic need to make this all fit. However, true scholars know that the real purpose of the four-grade middle school is to have younger students, age ten and eleven, also put their brains into lockdown—like the twelve- and thirteen-year-olds—lose all coordination, and get lost in their lockers earlier than they normally would.

But in 1981, junior highs, not middle schools, were the norm. At Norwalk Regional Junior High School, students came into contact, for the first time since kindergarten, with students not from their own neighborhood or town. Norwalk Junior High was, along with the King Metacomet High School, part of a regional school district involving three towns. King Metacomet, otherwise known by his English name of King Philip, waged war in the whole area from 1675-1676 and drove all the settlers out. But now, there was no memory of those battles; the three towns were bustling, bedroom suburbias with easy access to Boston and Providence.

There was Norwalk where the affluent lived. There you could have two-acre homesteads, look at beautiful scenery, live in the safety of the quiet, and catch the train to Boston. Wentam, where the middle class lived and enjoyed three beautiful lakes, was a three-hundred-year-old New England town whose center  proudly showed off her beautiful band-stand and the Congregational Church, which boastfully sup-ported a tall white steeple.  And there was Plaintown, the poorer stepsister which lacked any real center except for a tacky, miniscule variety store; there the kids hopped on the regional bus and rode for an hour to get to school.

My room at Norwalk Junior High was in-between the rooms of two other social-studies teachers.  Mr. Ballini, on the one side, taught U.S. history, and Mr. Stanton, on the other, taught cultural geography.  I taught a bit of both.  Mr. Ballini was a hard-nose, all-serious, all-consuming teacher.  His usual threat, "If you disturb my class, you will meet me in the gym after school," stopped everyone cold.  I never knew what went on in that gym. I think it was some kind of weird wrestling.

Mr. Stanton had a great sense of humor and constantly joked and interacted playfully with his students.  Only he could have gotten away with what he did that day he returned from being sick.  There had been a substitute teacher in his room and chaos had reigned.  A flimsy, temporary accordion wall was all that separated my room from Mr. Stanton's, and the noise and commotion in there that day disturbed all of my classes.  We accomplished nothing of value.  When I informed Mr. Stanton of his students' obnoxious behavior (and appar-ently the substitute had left him a scathing note as well), he sent each class, in groups of five, crawling on their hands and knees down the hall "like the slimy snakes they were" and in-to my room to apologize.  All day long the slimy snakes slith-ered down the hall. The last I knew, those slimy slithering snakes never interfered with a substitute again. And Mr. Stan-ton never got an office-invitational.  Why is that?

One day during that year, and it was now 1981 - 1982, Mr.

Stanton started shrieking, "Help me! Help me! Help me!" He sounded horrible; his cries got more and more frantic and louder and louder. I raced through the flimsy door in the flimsy accordion wall to see the most bizarre sight. Remember the old sixteen-millimeter film projectors where one wheel held the movie and the other was the uptake reel? Well, Mr. Stanton had gotten way too close as he was threading the film into that uptake reel and his tie had gotten caught in with the film and he couldn't get it loose. I flew back through the flimsy door in the flimsy accordion wall, trying not to laugh or scream out loud; grabbed my scissors; rushed back through the door; and, as the projector continued to whir and groan, cut Mr. Stanton's tie about two inches from his neck. I saved a life that day.

It is true that, just as dog owners start to resemble their dogs, teachers in junior highs and middle schools start to resemble their students and are never quite the same again. Teachers become as clumsy and as brainless as their charges. They lose their ability to walk right; they trip; they stumble; they fall into closets; they fall behind their desks; they bump into and fall over students' desks; they forget where they are going; they forget which classes are which; they get tangled up in the window blinds; they get their ties caught in uptake reels.

Meet some of the students.

There was Beth. Daily she emerged from the school bus a pretty, twelve-year-old girl looking cheerfully cherubic. Five minutes later in Mr. Ballini's homeroom, thanks to her hidden, multi-packet, makeup kit in her backpack, before the bell rang to announce the start of the day, she had turned herself into a twenty-five-year-old, not-so-angelic-looking model. That is how she pranced around the school. On the bus ride home, her makeup came off and when she exited the bus and ran into her house, her mom welcomed an unblemished, twelve-year-old girl back home. Her mom was so happy that Beth hadn't gotten into all that makeup and stuff the other girls had.

And there was Matt. He wasn't in any of my classes, but he was in my homeroom. Ah yes, homeroom. That is the bizarre limbo before the start of classes when and where no one knows what they are supposed to be doing. It's a place and time that promises to promote all kinds of odd goings-on among the twelve- and thirteen-year-old set. Matt was a quiet, well-behaved boy with a beautiful head of thick blond hair. One day he came into my homeroom in tears. I could tell by looking at him that something raucous and probably felonious had gone down on the school bus. Matt had ten or twenty large hunks of gum stuck, really stuck, in his hair all over the top of his head. Kids can be cruel. Twelve- and thirteen-year-olds can be strange, and hateful, and warped, and creative, and sweet, and mouthy, and mean, and kind, and just plain cruel. That is who they are.

My dilemma was what to do about Matt's hair. Should I send him to the nurse? What would she do? Send him for surgery? Attach a Band-Aid? Wrap him in gauze? Take his temperature? No, I decided, I would send him to Miss Ryan, the girls' gym teacher. She had solutions for everything.

"Matt, go down to the girls' gym and give this note to Miss Ryan. She will fix your hair," I instructed with total confidence in Miss Ryan's problem-solving abilities. The note explained the situation, as if Miss Ryan wouldn't grasp it just by looking, but it gave Matt something to hold onto.

"I have to go into the girls' gym?" he asked in dismay. "Everyone will laugh at me. Do I have to do that?"

"It will be okay, there is no one in the gym right now," I promised as I tried to reassure Matt; not that he was reassured at all.

Matt trudged down the hall with his eyes glued to the floor, a beaten person with his shoulders bent over as if he were heading to the gallows, never to return. He clung onto the note, his key to salvation. He came back in about fifteen minutes a new and different twelve-year-old, bouncing energetically into my room. He was sporting a Cheshire-Cat smile and a fashionable new crew cut. Miss Ryan, you rocked.

The brothers Grim. These were two brothers from Plaintown. But really, there are brothers Grim in every school, in every town, in every city. One was in the seventh grade; one was in the eighth grade. Their command of filthy language indicated that they came from a long line of family members who had fine-tuned one-syllable words, mostly beginning with "f" and "s" and "b" with an occasional "c" thrown in for good measure. They were a force with which to be reckoned and it wasn't a positive force. The younger one was in my homeroom and was always causing some kind of trouble. Together, they were the nastiest pair in the school, two noxious bullies. The older one failed all of his classes that year and so was going to be repeating eighth grade. This meant that both brothers would be in the eighth grade the following year. Teachers and students braced themselves.

I tried to be inventive with the students at Norwalk Junior High School. I think all that cerebral exertion was paying off; I think I had stepped up my teaching. The assignment in one of the geography classes was for each student to make a board game of professional caliber. It had to be a game which contained the board, the playing pieces, and the rules, and that demonstrated that they, the student game developers, understood a particular topic in geography. It might be a game about world migration or it might be a game about time zones. It could be about any interesting topic that lent itself to a game format. We submitted the best to game companies. Another assignment was for them to write a book appropriate for five- to eight-year-olds about an intriguing geographic subject. It might be a book about world fungi, including ergot of rye, or maybe it would be a book about tsunamis. The possibilities were endless. And we sent the best of those to publishers.

And one weekend homework task, arguably not nearly as inspired but with a potential to lead to an enthralling study of the Norsemen, was to watch the special PBS production on Saturday about the Vikings. That Saturday I watched the broadcast to be ready to discuss the show on Monday with the students. I watched spellbound, more spellbound, mesmerized, completely pleased with the assignment, and totally captivated, and then ... utterly horrified and more horrified and then hysterical as the show depicted rape after rape after rape.

What was wrong with me? Hadn't I learned anything from the *Travels with Charley* fiasco back in Milltown? Why had I been so careless as to assign a TV show I hadn't previewed? Did I really want another office-invitational? I was as dense as a thick brick. I dreaded going to school on Monday. This particular principal always wanted his teachers to notify him when there was even a remote possibility that a parent might get angry over something. He always wanted to be prepared. Should I tell Mr. King? Should I not tell him? Should I call in sick? Should I run away? Should I kill myself? I decided not to tell him. I dragged myself into school waiting for a deadly, volcanic eruption.

Class began. Hardly able to speak, I managed to spit out, "Raise your hand if you watched the PBS special on the Vikings on Saturday." I felt faint. I felt all the blood rush out of my face. I was definitely going to faint. I couldn't see. I was losing my vision; I was going blind. I was dying. ... Oh? Not one hand? The blood slowly returned to my face. Everything was in slow motion. I didn't faint. I felt my pulse; I had one. My hands had feeling in them again. I could see; it was a miracle. I lived. I had dodged a career-ending, canon-ball-size bullet. No one had watched the program. The moral of the story is that if you are going to assign a TV program that you haven't previewed, make sure it airs on a Saturday. No one will watch it.

Planning was a whole other thing at Norwalk. The principal required every teacher to fill out the next week's lesson plans, including homework assignments, and to deliver the plan book to him on the Friday of every week. What drudgery. Who could be flummoxed enough to think that teachers ever followed the plans they wrote? And who spent their weekends reviewing over fifty teachers' plan books? Who does that? And why?

I spent the whole year trying to circumvent that requirement. I tried reproducing parts, just changing page numbers and topics. That was an eyesore what with the white-outs, the cross-outs, and the write-overs. I tried forgetting to do it. That did not have a good outcome. Please, no more office-invitationals. I finally succumbed, did it, handed it in, and never looked at it once. I also promised myself if I ever became an administrator the only thing I would require of teachers would be that every plan be creative. If only teachers could be creative. I never became an administrator.

By early spring of 1982, the school budget was showing

signs of panic and depletion. Proposition 2½ was about to go into effect and all schools would be losing money from their budgets. And at that time, in Massachusetts, the teacher contracts promised that if the school district thought there might not be enough money to rehire a teacher the following September, the district had to send a warning *pink-slip* to that teacher by early spring or the school had to retain the teacher automatically. It was a spring ritual. This year, Norwalk sent these pink notices, which weren't really pink, to all of the teachers it had hired in September of 1981, including me. And in June, I said good-bye to Norwalk Junior High and left the brothers Grim behind. It was not the last I would hear of them.

Meanwhile, a lot had been happening in Woburn, twenty miles to the north. After that 1979 meeting at Rev. Young's church had revealed that there was an aggregation of leukemia cases in Anne Anderson's neighborhood (which wells G and H served), at the request of Jimmy Anderson's doctor—Dr. John Truman of Massachusetts General Hospital—the CDC in Atlanta had initiated a study to investigate and to determine if this cluster had anything to do with the water.

Five days after Jimmy Anderson died in January of 1981, the CDC published the results of their investigation which revealed that the number of cases of leukemia in that part of Woburn was unusually high compared with the national rate, and that the incidence of leukemia was seven times greater than what one would have expected. Poisoned water was the main suspect. The EPA was conducting its own research, and while that continued, on April 5, 1982,—at about the same time that I received my pink slip—eight families, including the Andersons, filed a lawsuit against the three companies they thought responsible for the contamination.

*Anne Anderson et al. v. W.R. Grace et al.* was to become a classic David and Goliath story. It was the eight Woburn families, each suffering from the tragedy of losing a child, against Unifirst, the industrial dry-cleaning company; against W.R. Grace, which owned and operated the Cryovac manufacturing plant which used solvents to clean its tools, cut grease, and dilute paint; and against Beatrice Foods, co-owner of the J.J. Riley Tannery, the only tannery left in Woburn. The case wouldn't come to trial for four years.

## Chapter 11

## Boot Camp

Sort of like the emperor with no clothes, a substitute teacher thinks she is dressed, but really she has no armor, no training, no weaponry and has to face approximately thirty-five cunning combatants, each period, who see clearly that she is missing these things and who are waiting to joyfully eliminate her or at least reduce her to a sniveling shell of a person. I have seen even retired military officers—trying to substitute teach in junior highs, middle schools, and high schools— collapse in tears.  The military retirees, who are used to squawking orders and having obedient soldiers jump to their commands, have no similar power in a classroom.  They can spit out all the orders they want.  They can't send anyone to the brig or take away anyone's pay.  The best they or any other substitute teacher can do is, as an example, send the hooligan(s) or goof-ball(s) to the office.  It is not a pretty sight watching thirty-five students annihilate a perfectly normal and conscientious human being.

But I already knew a lot of the students in this school system so I jumped into subbing, since I couldn't find any other work, without a lot of trepidation. Much to my surprise, though, none of my assignments were at the junior high. They were all at the high school where I was relatively unknown and where I was extraordinarily busy.  For the first six weeks, I replaced a library assistant on sick leave.  This is when I met Emmelyn, the library's director, and it is when I gained valuable insights into the role and importance of a library.  It was also when I learned that a librarian can save your life.

There was a strange thing going on in the library. I wondered why I kept seeing students, who I knew weren't into reading, come into the library during their study periods. They all headed down the aisle with books on art, architecture, and design. I decided to traipse down that row one day during a lull. I pulled out a few books trying to figure out what the attraction was. There were very large art books with photos and drawings of naked humans. (This was not the South; the King Metacomet School Committee hadn't banned these books.) Was that the seduction? Whoa, when I opened the sixth or seventh book, fifty dollars fell out. A short investigation later, we discovered a prolific, student drug-ring in the school. The drug-buying students were putting money in the art book—and probably enjoying the views as they did it—and waiting for the drug-dealing peers to replace the money with packets of drugs. High school students can be very shrewd.

Once the library position ended, the high school called me for daily classroom subbing. Every class that walked, jumped, sprinted, or fell in through the doorway was a different dynamic. Thinking fast on my feet was not enough. I had to be diabolical, I had to have multiple contingency plans, and always I had to have a means, and a road by which, to retreat.

Things were going okay, by which I mean I was still standing, still able to speak, could still see and hear, had no new scars, and was still physically intact. Then I had to sub for Mr. Lattaro, the science teacher all the students worshipped. It was a large class of seniors who looked pretty friendly. Mr Lattaro had not left any instructions for a sub, so I had to punt. I asked the students what book they were using and I got five different answers. Soooo, they were going to be ditsy and play the *beat-us-if-you-can* game. Okay. I know how to do that. I positioned myself as close as I could to a student in the front seat, side row.  My back was to the rest of the students and this student couldn't see anything past me.  Isolation and close proximity are powerful tools in classroom management.  "Which book does this class use, Karen," I asked, "and where are you in it?"  She gave it up instantly.

That didn't mean they were going to cooperate with me.  I assigned them a chapter to read and they just sat there, ignoring me; they continued to chat with each other.  Then a group of five got up and started out the door.

"Wait a minute!  Where are you going?" I questioned them.

"To the lav," Jake answered.

"You need to go one at a time and you need a pass."

"Not in here we don't.  Mr. Lattaro doesn't make us do that.  He says we're not babies."

This no-rules process may have been working for Mr. Lattaro, but it sure didn't work for a sub.

"While I am here, you have to follow my directions," I asserted. "Come up and get a slip, and you may go one at a time."

They ignored me and walked out of the room.  When they came back halfway through the period, I called the office on the intercom, explained the situation to Mr. Shapiro, the vice principal, and then sent the freely-floating-five to visit him.  Two more students refused my directions and they took the same trip.  The school never asked me to sub for Mr. Lattaro again.  I finally figured it out.  Feigned or real incompetence works every time; if you want to get out of doing something, be really bad at doing it.

Then that one day there was the big fifth-period class for students from the vocational wing.  These students only came into the main high school for U.S. history and English classes.  The U.S. history class, for which I was subbing, was another lunch splitting class—part of the class before lunch, part of the class after—but with a twist. There were so many kids in this high school that each fifth period had four segments in order to accommodate all the students in the cafeteria. It went class, lunch, class, and then more class or study time or some variation of these four time frames.

I was ready at my sentry-door post when thirty hulking young men burst into my room. They were afraid of nothing, least of all me. Within seconds they had rearranged the room, while I was still dutifully at my station. They had whipped out playing cards and were playing polka in groups of four. Thinking of all the inventive sharp objects they had probably made and smuggled in from the vocational building, I fearfully entered the room and, like the wimp I was, squeaked with the voice of a mouse, "Are you going to hurt me?"

Their apparent spokesperson replied, "No, we won't." For whatever reason, I believed them. They were concentrating on their polka games. Now what? What should I do? They were in control. ... Suddenly, in an epiphanic flash, it came to me. Call down to Emmelyn and beg for help. Emmelyn knew everything that was in the library. She would know what to do. And I was right. Within minutes she appeared at my room with a video player and videotape ready to go. I didn't even ask what it was. She said it would work; I believed her. Emmelyn, just like Ms. Ryan at the junior high, knew everything.

I set it in front of the class, plugged in the machine, and pressed *play*. If you were the media specialist, what videotape would you have chosen for these brawny hulks who knew how to build, plumb, and electrify houses? What would you have done?

The videotape began and suddenly the playing cards flew back into their packages. The students re-set the desks and chairs to face the machine, and for the rest of that part of class and for the rest of the class time after lunch, they watched, mesmerized and glued to the screen. Why? Because it was an hour and a half of National Geographic's videotape of African natives, wearing loincloths or nothing at all, busy with their daily chores. And nobody complained. Nobody spoke. They were riveted. Always think National Geographic.

Times had certainly changed since the Milltown principal, Mr. Hawn, had reprimanded me for having students read *Travels with Charley* with its unacceptable language. Here were students watching nude women and men cavorting throughout their villages. From that point on, subbing became a rather wonderfully playful and positive repartee between me and them, whoever they were, as long as Emmelyn was in my back pocket.

While I was subbing in the high school, that year of 1982-1983, my child who had survived the water of Woburn and the Boston busing experiment, entered Norwalk Junior High. One day in October, just four months after I had left that school and a month after he had entered it, he returned home from school looking strangely distraught. The ensuing conversation went like this:

I: "How did things go today at school?"

He: "Good, until I went into the boys' lav."

I: "What happened in there?"

He: "Two brothers cornered me."

*I knew it. The brothers Grim.*

I (fearfully and apprehensively): "What happened?"

He: "They said, 'Your mother is a bitch.'"

I (trying to remain calm): "And what did you do?"

He: "I had to think really fast so they wouldn't kill me and I did and said, 'Well, if you think she is a bitch in school, you should try to live with her.'"

*#&%!!&$#&*!   He had saved his own life. I didn't know whether to applaud his creativity and fast thinking in avoiding a certain physical pummeling or to wring his neck. I chose to celebrate his cleverness. He lived after all.

And on went my year of subbing at the high school, always with Emmelyn as my sidekick. Mostly I was busy looking for that next job.

## Chapter 12

## Second Choice at Blackstone and Dynamite

One thing I really liked about this career I hadn't actually chosen was her unpredictability. And Blackstone High School did not disappoint; the school dished out unpredictability in reams. The interview with the unlikely, odd pair of the principal and vice principal at Blackstone High School was just plain strange. Principal LeBlanc, a former noble jock who double dipped as the radio announcer for the Friday-night football games, and Vice Principal McCarthy, a defector from a Catholic seminary, were all business. They kept returning to the same matter and took turns grilling me.

Mr. LeBlanc: "What do you think is the most important part of classroom management?"

Mr. McCarthy: "What kind of classroom management problems have you had in the past?"

Mr. LeBlanc: "What is the biggest problem you have had?"

Mr. McCarthy: "What are your approaches to classroom management?"

"I have never had a problem managing a class," I answered firmly. "It's all about being proactive and preemptive. It's pretty simple," I smugly responded. They didn't have to know about Kevin or the cafeteria study hall at Milltown.

Then I started doing the asking.

"Why is there an opening in January?"

"Did the teacher get sick?"

"Is she on maternity leave?"

"Were there discipline problems in her classes?"

"Oh, no, no, no. No discipline problems. The teacher became ill and had to leave," Mr. LeBlanc assured me.

What the administration neglected to tell me was that Ms. Honig, the teacher, had had a nervous breakdown in trying to deal with one particular class. That was mine to discover on my first day of classes.

The interview with the social-studies chairperson, Mr Caski, was almost as weird, but he didn't care about the class-room-management factor. He had a message to deliver and he did as he blurted out, "I will hire you, if you pass the super-intendent's scrutiny, but I want you to know that you are my second choice. My first choice declined the offer." Whatever compelled him to tell me that, I have no idea. Maybe it was to keep me in check and to show me who was boss. I don't know.

Next was the interview with the superintendent, Mr. Carter, a big, bulky man. Really, could things get any more peculiar? He was aloof; there was no eye contact; and he paced all over the room. Proudly like a peacock, in a big booming voice, he explained his theory of a cost-effective school policy and it was a lollapalooza: *The less a teacher gets paid, the harder she works.* Did he stay up nights dreaming up this cockamamie scheme? Apparently not. He contended he had done the research. I couldn't make up this stuff. By this time, unions in Massachusetts had made some inroads into better pay and better schedules, but evidently not in Blackstone. And with an overabundance of teachers looking for work, this big-bulky-superintendent-rooster was ruling the roost.

I had learned how strong the union was at Norwalk after I had neglected to join it, then had asked my colleagues—via notes in their mailboxes—to help me with some research. My car had paid the price for that indiscretion; but at least that union had spunk. The union at Blackstone, on the other hand, was a wishy-washy, lack-luster group. I think Mr. Carter probably had a lot to do with that. It lay at his feet, as probably did the school committee. It is the school superintendent in Massachusetts who develops and writes the school budget, and Mr. Carter had probably strong-armed both the Blackstone School Committee and the Blackstone Teachers' Union into accepting his innovative, repressive, regressive plan. Later, when I became one of the teachers' representatives to the union and tried to speak during a meeting with the school committee, their—the school's—lawyer promptly and loudly dismissed and verbally accosted me and told me in no uncertain terms to shut up. Only one person was steering this ship and that was Mr. Carter.

"Take it or leave it," Mr. Carter declared bluntly to me. "First-step pay."

Well! ... How *insulting!* How *humiliating*! How *demeaning*! No wonder Mr. Caski's preferred candidate had declined the job. But, I had no bargaining power. I was already, and obviously, not the top prize (at least not for Mr. Caski) and that glut of teachers was nowhere bigger than in the field of social studies. A dime a dozen. The only thing I had going for me was my gender. As I had been in Woburn, I was the only female who had applied for this job and schools were still paying attention to civil-rights and affirmative-action protocol.

So, I did what I had to do. I accepted the proposition, which is what it felt like, and went immediately to the jeweler's to buy a silver chain. And from that chain I hung only one charm, a silver #2. I didn't want to get a big head. And with my new jewelry adorning my neck and reminding me what and who I was, I started my unforeseen career all over again with a first-year teacher's pay. The good news was that I no longer had to worry about teaching that economics class in my schedule. I could spend the whole semester on the concept of supply and demand.

Let's face it, this had been an erratic trail to this point—two years at Milltown, one year at Glenridge, two years in Woburn, one year with Norwalk, and one year of subbing at King Metacomet. Maybe this was my chance to stay awhile in one place and to really get to know the students and the school community. Maybe it was the time to use all those lesson plans that were living in my head, rent free, before they started to leak out. Maybe it was my opportunity to finally figure out how the heck to teach, for real.

While I was sorting all that out, the evening news continued to keep me close to Woburn, thirty-five miles to the northeast. On February 9, 1984, a month after I started at Blackstone, there was yet another scary report. The Harvard School of Public Health released their three-year study of leukemia in Woburn. They found, similarly to the CDC, that the water from wells G and H was significantly linked to a variety of adverse health effects including childhood leukemia, fetal and new-born deaths, and several birth defects. How would these findings impact the trial, I wondered.

The Andersons and the other litigants were still waiting for that trial to begin, while I was figuring out where I was. Where was I? Blackstone was a completely different town from Woburn. If you like pastoral countryside, you would like Blackstone. It is a bucolic little New England town where people have abundant land; where people own, ride, and train horses; where the 4H Club is alive and well; where everyone knows everyone. It is beautifully green. You can smell the green. Unlike Milltown which is right next door, Blackstone was never a mill town. And unlike Woburn, it was never a working-class town. This was the upscale, desirable, bedroom community. It was a beautiful place to work.

My classroom, similar to the one in Milltown had been, was at the end of a crossover bridge connecting two buildings. But, instead of leading to other classrooms, as the bridge had in Milltown, it took the students to the gym, the auditorium, the cafeteria, and the woodworking shop; and, have mercy, I did not have door-peg duty. Apparently, the students at Blackstone knew how to open doors.

At the time, a lot of secondary schools were experimenting with rotating schedules. This meant that you never had the same class at the same time in a grouping of five to seven days. Norwalk Junior High had had a six-day rotating schedule. I hated it. I could never tell by which day it was, what class would tumble in next. I didn't know whether to prepare for the noisiest or the quietest or the worst-behaved or the best-behaved or the unprepared or the most prepared or the crankiest or the friendliest.

The schedule at Norwalk didn't repeat every Monday; oh, no, it went from Monday to the next Tuesday; then Tuesday to the next Wednesday and so on. At the end of every class period, I had to walk to the taped-up schedule on the blackboard to see who would be coming through the door and in what condition. I was rotating-schedule challenged. I never did figure out how the students always knew where they were going, especially in a place where things always go the wrong way.

So, I was glad when I learned that Blackstone High School was still sticking to the traditional routine which would mean the same class, at the same time, every day. There was something comforting about knowing what I was doing and when. But there was also something different at Blackstone. Instead of having a study hall or a cafeteria study, students would return to their home classroom when it was time for their study period and sit at the back of the room while the teacher taught whatever class was in there at the time. There were usually six or seven students sitting in the back of every class. It seemed like a peculiar set-up to me, but it actually worked pretty well. The students never made a ruckus back there. That didn't mean they were studying or doing anything constructive, but I didn't care about that, as long as they didn't disturb my class.

That all changed one day when Richard, at the back of the room, had some kind of outrageous fit and threatened to throw his one-piece desk-chair out the window of my second-story room. He did smash the window with the bottom of the desk, but, thankfully, didn't throw the awkward, heavy missile out. I had a flash vision of someone walking outside below, and a ninety-pound wooden desk suddenly crashing down on his head.

The standoff went something like this:

I: "Richard, put the desk down slowly, please, and head to the office."

He stood there with his weapon, the combo desk-chair, raised about to his waist.

He (yelling): "*No!*"

I: "Go to the office, please."

He: "*Make me!*"

Now he was sparring with me?

I (for the third time): "Richard, go to the office, please."

He (yelling, again): "*I am not going to the office! You can't make me!*"

I (walking towards the intercom): "Richard, you have two choices. You can put your desk down and walk to the office, or I can call the office and have the principal come and get you. Which do you want?"

This time Richard slammed the desk-chair down with some kind of primitive grunt and with as loud a thud as he could manage. He stomped around the back of the room and down the side aisle to the door where he knocked his elbow through the door's window, opened the door while the broken glass fell all over him and all over the floor, sprinted out of the room, and flew Mr. Carter's coop. By the time I notified the office, Richard was long gone. That cafeteria study at Milltown, that had caused me so much angst, and the study hall at Glenridge, with all the black-leather jackets blocking the passageway, didn't seem so bad anymore. There was no breaking of glass in those study sessions.

Aside from this petulant display, things went pretty well. I liked and looked forward to my hodgepodge schedule. There was plenty of diversity—two sophomore world-civilization classes, my favorite; two freshman U.S. history classes, my least favorite; and several different one semester subjects that would rotate over a two-year period. This included economics, psychology, sociology, and law. With my newfound knowledge about supply and demand, I was ready for the economics; and my college background had prepared me for sociology and psychology. Law? I was learning right along with the students, just as I had done with the Spanish classes at Milltown. But, thankfully, this class was in English. .

The law class was like having explosives all around me and inside me. There wasn't enough time to do everything that was popping into my head. My brain was blasting in every direction. It was spitting out ideas as fast as the candy rolled down the conveyer belt in the old *I-Love-Lucy* classic. At least now I had someplace to use all the notions. We had already had an excursion into tenets of the law when we debated the rights of students to privacy in regard to their lockers. That had everyone engaged or enraged; it depended on the day.

Then there was a point during that semester that the students were ready to mutiny over my grading system. Ah, Ha! Perfect. We would have a mock trial. I would be the defendant, and the class would file a class action against me. The students would develop and walk through this legal process from start to finish.

To begin, students drew slips out of a hat and whatever they picked told them what role they would research and play. There would be the judge, the prosecutor's team, the defense attorney's team, the jurors, the witnesses for both sides, the transcriber, the bailiff. And prepare they did. I knew it could turn into a mob rule with me heading to the torture chamber; that was one possibility. Or it might turn out to be a learning experience extraordinaire; it could. Or it might just be a complete flop.

Sarah, a quite attractive, but disenfranchised, hostile and angry, seventeen-year-old young woman, did not have a friend in this class or anywhere else that I could tell. She sat at the back of the room, seemingly disinterested in everything in the class and in life in general. Her disaffected expression never changed. She did her work most of the time, but it was poor at best. As luck or misfortune would have it, she drew the slip that said *judge*. Now I was worried about the whole experiment disintegrating.

I fretted for nothing. Sarah sprang to life. She became a self she hadn't even met before. She did voluminous amounts of research. She searched for similar cases with the help of Marion, Blackstone High School's fabulous librarian. She investigated the role of a judge. In front of a mirror, she practiced how she would speak. She rehearsed the demeanor she would have. It would be serious. She thought about what she

85

would wear. It would be a suit. She would pull her hair back to look professional. She watched movies about criminal trials. She had found her voice; she had found Sarah.

And throughout the trial, which lasted several days, she was as professional in her position as any real judge would have been. She never wavered; she never showed uncertainty. She was completely objective. She didn't favor one side or the other. She was clear in her rulings when there were objections. "Overruled!" "Overruled!" "Sustained!" "Approach the bench." And if anyone in her court disrupted the proceedings for any reason or in any way, in the blink of an eye, her gavel came down loudly and swiftly and she handed down whatever punishment she deemed fit. She took care of it steadfastly and with the authority of a long-time judge.

"Out of my courtroom!" she bellowed if someone laughed. "Bailiff, escort those two people out of the courtroom," she ordered when two people in her court were chatting. "Another outburst and this court will find you in contempt," she said as she stared at one of the witnesses. "I find you in contempt of court. Thirty days in jail. Bailiff, ... " and on it went.

We needed two trials. The first was a hung jury. The second trial, with the students playing all new roles, found me guilty of applying an oppressive grade system. The new judge, Rob, did a fine job, but he couldn't hold a candle to Sarah. Next came the sentencing phase. Thankfully, they didn't send me to jail. They decided on something very useful to them. The court laid down a punishment that required me to allow the class to develop their own grading system as long as it had a reasonable and supporting rationale; additionally, I could not impose homework for two weeks. I got off easy.

Once again, I could feel the stirring in the brain brewery. It was that same kind of strange, brief headache I had had when

I had learned that my friend Allan was missing in Vietnam, and when I had learned about the contaminated water in the Woburn wells, and when I was living through the fury of forced busing in Boston, and when I watched the students at the football games. But this time the brewing seemed more widespread and felt almost like massive, uncontrollable waves crashing in my head. What had I learned about teaching and learning from all this? Could it be? Could it be that students learn best when lessons come from experiences, the teacher's and the students'? Could it be that students learn more when a lesson is connected to real life events? Could it be that students are more engaged when actively involved?

In retrospect, I realize that it was sometime during my time at Blackstone that the brewing had turned to fermenting and distilling; I think I was getting to the meat of things.

## Chapter 13

## Ataxia and Rethinking It All

Speaking of unpredictability, for the U.S. history classes, there was a new and interesting experiment which had begun the previous September. The department chairperson, Mr. Caski, the very one, who, after all, was responsible for my wearing the #2 around my neck every day, had similar issues to the ones I had with the disconnect between the eighth-grade half and the eleventh- or twelfth-grade part of U.S. history. So, in his genius, he decided we would teach that second half of U.S. history in the ninth grade.

There was only one problem; actually there were two problems. First, book publishers are all about money. And the way they make money is to publish books that entire states, rather than individual teachers, adopt and require in all their schools, in all their classes. Twenty-one states, mostly in the South and in the West, are adoption states, meaning that the state controls which books either get into schools or onto a recommended list from which districts may choose. States like Texas and Alabama—whose books sometimes lean to the Christian and far Right—with a combined total of over six million students, determine, in large measure, which books publishers publish because it is guaranteed money for them.

The second problem is that all of the U.S. history books are geared to eleventh and twelfth grade students because that is when students take U.S. history in most secondary schools and definitely in Texas and Alabama. Most ninth graders aren't really ready to understand the concepts that juniors and seniors can so all of the books were a problem.

A few weeks after I started at Blackstone, quite by chance, I received a desk copy of a book called *The American Dream* by Lew Smith. It was a Scott, Foresman & Co. publication. As soon as I reviewed it, I knew I had found a book that would be exactly right for my U.S. history classes. This book was full of investigative inquiries the students could conduct. It encouraged students to gather, analyze, and review information and to draw conclusions. It required students to think! I was excited and looking forward, for the first time, to teaching U.S. history. But It would have to wait until the next academic year. For my first semester at Blackstone, I had to use the books the ninth-grade students had started the year with in September.

Ah, yes, return with me to that first day of classes. I wasn't exactly honest when I said things were going well. There was one exception. On that first day, the first four groups were very large, pretty much thirty-five in every class, but nothing stuck out as unusual. Eventually, it was time for my last class of the day in the last period of the seven-period day. Only seventeen students were in the class. I was so glad this was a traditional schedule and that my last class of every day would be this perfect size.

Wham! Bam! All hell broke loose as the students propelled themselves into the room. Jay, the first student, dashed in, jumped onto a chair, then to another, and another, and another, all while flicking his BiC lighter so that the flame was about eight inches high. The rest galloped into the room in a helter-skelter fashion pushing and shoving, knocking over desks, and creating such a noise that it was a miracle they didn't hear it in the main office on the floor below. Maybe they had heard it; maybe they had heard it last semester and were now just ignoring it. Everything went downhill from there. It was a frenzied, convulsive, maniacal bedlam.

And in an instant I knew. I knew why Ms. Honig had left in December. I knew why she had become *ill.* It wasn't her problem anymore, it was mine. Well, Ms. Smarty Pants who had never had a problem with classroom management, now what? And how do you feel now about having a non-rotating, fixed schedule? Wouldn't it be great dealing with this class at the end of every day?

I was back in the principal's office that afternoon asking what the heck was the deal with this class. And finally I got answers to the questions I had asked at the job interview. Of the seventeen students, fourteen had IEPs, individualized education programs; all had different needs, of course. Some had learning disabilities. Some had various behavior or emotional issues in different degrees. Some had a combination of problems, but no combinations were the same. By law there should have been a special-education aide in the room, but there wasn't. I blamed it on Mr. Carter and his obsessive, penny-pinching ways and his warped theory of educational appropriation.

This was one of my two U.S. history classes; the students were freshmen using the book that was meant for juniors and seniors, never mind that most of these students could barely read, let alone comprehend or care. One horrible day followed another. Daily I confiscated BiCs. Daily I had to take away various kinds of weapons—knives, cords, belts, anything with which Joey could poke someone, Patrick's keys that he rattled and threw around, Mark's piece of chain, Tony's green water pistol. Every day I had to take cigarettes away from Brendan; he would come into class wearing a couple of them stuck to his lips. Every ten minutes or so, Nate got up and roamed around the room. Steve would let out a blood-curdling, high-pitched shriek every few minutes. And then the day came, when at the very end of my rope, after trying everything I had known to work but in this class wasn't making a microscopic dent, I had another one of my splendid, smashing ideas.

The three students in the class without IEPs were very quiet and always looked terrified. They sat side-by-side in the front row. I decided, since they were the only ones paying attention or following directions or behaving appropriately, that I would consider them the only students in the class and work with just them. I would deport the other fourteen to the back two rows of the room and consider them exiles. I would ignore them. The only way they could get back *into* the class would be to behave impeccably back there for at least two weeks, and only then could they ask for permission to return.

My underlying assumption, probably faulty from the get-go, was that they would *want* to be back in the class. My main worry was that one of the administrators, in particular Mr. Carter, who loved to wander the halls and peer into classrooms, would be sneaking around, would peak through my door's window, and demand to know why most of the students were sitting in the back of the room. I really would have had no coherent explanation. I couldn't have said, "Because I can't stand any of them." I wouldn't have dared to say, "They're all delinquents (they weren't, but that is what it felt like)." And no way would I have asked, "Got any better ideas?" These responses wouldn't have worked well. Something worse than an office-invitational would have befallen me.

The first day of the experiment, I spent half of the class period explaining what was going to happen and why. One by one I excommunicated the fourteen perpetrators. They outnumbered me. There could have been a mutiny. They could have lit the classroom on fire with their BiCs; it could have been a bonfire. They could have had guns and wounded me. They could have stood their ground and refused to move. They could have laughed in my face and spat at me.

"Jack, sit in the back seat next to the windows."

"Brendan, sit next to Jack."

"Darren, sit next to Brendan." On it went and back they went: Zack, Butch, Patrick, Joey, Mack, Anthony, Steve, Casey, Jay, Brian, and Nate. All young men. I think they were in shock. Like leaderless sheep, they went obediently one at a time and sat there in back, silent for the rest of the period. I acted as if the three students up front were my entire class and as if nothing at all had happened. What did you say? There are fourteen students in the back of the room? Where?

The next few days, this group of chronic and incorrigible troublemakers came quietly into the room and went right away to their seats at the back. I was waiting for a massive outburst or for unimaginable terrorist acts or for constant interruptions or for fights to erupt. None of it happened. That made me more nervous than if it had. They were probably plotting the biggest takeover in the history of American education.

About two weeks later, the first of the ostracized expatriates approached me at the beginning of the class and asked if he could return. We had a serious talk about behavior boundaries, made a verbal contract regarding his conduct, and my class grew to four students. At the end of a month, they were all back in the class with the understanding that their presence in the class was a temporary status. "Misbehave and back you go," I warned them. I could seize and hold their visas at any time.

About halfway through the semester, Nate, already sixteen and still a freshman, and who had gotten two young women at the school pregnant, was arrested for stealing a car, and that reduced my class to sixteen. If I could survive long enough, my thinking went, maybe they would all self-eliminate.

The baggage these kids carried to school with them every day would have filled the luggage holds of at least a couple of airplanes, and this baggage included disadvantaged or abusive home lives, missing parents, alcoholic parents, intellectually-challenged parents, incarcerated parents, mental illness in the family, poverty, neglect. (No, living in sophisticated suburbia doesn't exclude these issues.) The most I could do for them was to provide and maintain a safe classroom, whether they wanted it or not. So, in the end, there was very little learning about U.S. history in this class.

I doubt these students could tell anyone much about even one important episode in our history. They probably don't know the difference between the Civil War and World War II or between Franklin D. Roosevelt and Dwight D. Eisenhower or between suffragettes and slaves. We spent a lot of the time learning how to use *please* and *thank you* and other civilized expressions. We spent a month learning about the words *cooperate* and *appropriate* (as in behavior). So much for academics. What I discovered was that sometimes it was more important—for me, for the students, and for society—to teach about behavior than it was to teach about history.

The good news was that I did manage to finish that semester with me and all my students still alive, without any major incidents, without Mr. Carter spying, and without any parent complaining. But I was exhausted. Was this really the place for me? I hadn't wanted to be a teacher in the first place. This was so much work. This was too much work. This kind of intense labor had never been in my plans. If I had to do something this demanding, why not become a CEO and make a lot of money. Not only was I responsible for one hundred and fifty teenagers every day from 7:30 a.m. to 2:30 p.m., but then I drove forty miles back home to confront two teenagers and one pre-teen of my own. I had three dependents to chauffer hither and yon every afternoon. Schlepping. Hadn't I ever heard of *planning* parenthood? Didn't I understand that these three children would be three college students in a few years and we would be bankrupt? I digress. I was very tired. This class had wrung me out like a piece of dripping, wet laundry. They might as well have put me through the wringer of Mom's antique washing machine.

I needed to take the summer to rethink the whole darn thing. And I did. And it was late in August when I saw an article in the local newspaper recounting the dramatic experiences of high-school students who had participated during the past year as contestants in the National History Day program.

I knew the students in this article. They were local teenagers, some were friends of my own children. They were not topnotch students; they were rather average, I-hate-school, I-would-rather-do-anything-than-go-to-school, history-is-so-boring kind of kids. And here they were talking to a reporter and recounting how thrilling they found both this program and, much to their own surprise, history.

Jane declared, "It's the best thing I've ever done in school."

Bob claimed, "It's the only time I have actually liked history."

And Karen suggested, "All our classes should be like this."

Right then I made a deal with myself and the academic devil: I would find out all I could about this program and enroll my students in it next year. If, at the end of the year, I and my students weren't as enthralled with history as these students in the newspaper were, that would be my final year. I would become a computer whiz, or a foreign diplomat or an engi-neer or a real-estate agent or a dental assistant or an x-ray technician or a car mechanic or I would create my own travel company or...

## Chapter 14

## A Deal with the Devil, a Student Teacher, and Falling Short

That next year at Blackstone I kept having intra-brain colli-
sions. It was my old brain jousting with the new emerging
brain. The new ideas about teaching adolescents were plow-
ing into the old ones or into the vacant space where there had
been nothing in the first place. The waves and the headaches I
had experienced intermittently when I knew something positive and productive and intense was happening with the students at Milltown or Glenridge or Woburn or Norwalk and
even while subbing in the boot camp at King Metacomet High
School were now evolving into a more consistent kind of per-
cussive jolts. It was annoying to say the least, having shocks
in my brain while I was trying to do things. It was sort of like
the irritation I felt when my second son, the drummer, tapped
with his fingers on the kitchen table, on the arm of the sofa, on
the back of my seat in the car, on the floor of his bedroom, on
his sister's head. Annoying. Dissonance.

There was a lot to put together that Fall of 1984. One really
good thing had happened during the summer. Mr. Caski, the
department chairperson, had forsaken teaching to open a coffee shop. I didn't quite get that particular segue; it wouldn't
have been my first-choice egress, but a bit later in my unantic-
ipated career, maybe I would understand it. I still wore my
#2 necklace every day just in case he reappeared.

The new chairperson was an eighth-grade teacher holding
court in the junior high school. It was fine with me that she
was in a different building. She did, though, give me the job
of updating the high school, social-studies curriculum. Just

like that. "Okay, Marilyn, you will be rewriting the curriculum for us and we have to see the new version at our next meeting. Thanks, see you all next month." And that was that.

Now someone thought I was the only one capable of writing curriculum? What had just happened? It took me a long time to realize that the more experienced teachers, the ones on tenure, just stood their ground and declined these extracurricular jobs.

Write curriculum? How do you do that? Where do you begin? What is curriculum? Is it a list of books? Is it the sequence of course work? Is it the courses themselves? I had no idea. I took the old curriculum, made some brief changes, and substituted the new book, *The American Dream,* for the old U.S. history books. This was the same ploy I had tried at Norwalk with my plan book. Just take one thing out, replace it with another. "Hello Everyone, here is your new program in social studies. Stop. No need for applause." Nobody cared. No one looked at it. Everyone did what they wanted to do in their classes.

*The American Dream* book turned out to be everything I had hoped it would be. It was chuck full of primary documents: hundreds of quotations from various and diverse origins; newspaper articles; art; political cartoons; photographs; posters; comics; movies; music; and more—all pulled together and available in one place. There were case studies, time lines, maps, and charts. It was a book that realized the relevance of many and varied sources and the radical importance of students forming their own opinions and conclusions. Novel. Genius. Engaging. A dream, indeed.

While the book contained the usual textbook questions about historical information, it went way beyond being an exercise in recall as it asked students to use all those data and details to think about and respond to heady and higher-level questions such as:

> *What is your personal definition of liberty?*
> *What factors seem to have determined whether or not an immigrant found life better in America?*
> *In what ways do your school and community represent a melting pot?*
> *A pluralistic society?*
> *Judging from photographs and posters from World War I, how did Americans at home react to the war effort?*

In addition, the book contained a treasure trove of activities that were complex and required an array of approaches and skills:

> *Interview an elected official about a particular subject.*
> *Write a newspaper article about 'My Life as a Slave.'*
> *Draw a cartoon depicting a problem in America that needs to be solved.*
> *Write a scene that takes place in the home of an immigrant Mexican family discussing whether or not to return to Mexico.*
> *Create posters supporting or attacking American control of Puerto Rico.*

On and on. Endless. For the first time, teaching U.S. history was not a chore.

But what I really wanted to do was try this NHD program with the world-history students. Beginning in September, students would choose a topic, a question, or a problem from world history; conduct research, the more primary the better; analyze, interpret, and organize the data; place it in historical context; and develop presentations on the topic. This was no insignificant feat for students who thought of history as a bunch of dreadfully boring information and who had no idea what secondary, let alone primary, research was.

And this was no trivial program. There were over half a

million students nation-wide who participated every year. There were intra-school competitions, then district contests, then the state rivalry, and finally, in June, the national championship at the University of Maryland. Most of the research and presentation preparation occurred from September to December. In the spring term the competitions would take place. My job was to have all of this work transpire while simultaneously addressing Blackstone's world-history curriculum. And if that didn't work, I would just alter the curriculum next year to make it fit the program. Better yet, I would make the NHD program the curriculum. Nobody would even notice.

I had ninety students altogether in the two world-history classes and the one economics class that would participate, so to make this manageable, I required the  students to work in groups of up to five in either the table-top or media category. The table-top setup was pretty self-explanatory and looked manageable enough as a group endeavor. Each table-top project would have three panels of a specific size that would include work demonstrating analysis, multiple perspectives, and context.

The media presentation would have to be a slideshow (my decision) like the one I had seen at the end of the school year the previous June. Mr Clausan, one of the social-studies teachers, had put together a synchronized show for the graduating seniors. Music and all. It was insanely awesome. So Mr. Clauson taught me how to use the sync machine; how to sync the slides with music; how to use two slide projectors with slides merging into each other; and how to come out with a show extraordinaire. This was the hands-on-real-deal with the real equipment, real slides. There were no easy slideshows or syncing of music on a computer in 1984.

Those first weeks of school were heavily into explaining the program, deciding who would be in what group, and what they would study. Already the energy level was an improvement over the previous semester. But what participating in this program meant was that we all had to spend hours after school in order to learn how to use the machines and create board projects. This didn't go smoothly. Some students wouldn't stay, some couldn't stay, and some just didn't care, period. We also had to spend hours in the library, and once again, Marion, Blackstone's fabulous librarian, rescued us.

She had the list of our topics and she consolidated appropriate piles of books to save us time. And we took bus trips to libraries that held special related collections. This included, for some of the students, the trip to the JFK library in Boston where again the librarian was ready for us and invaluable to the students and their understanding of research. For others, the Worcester Public Library, which held many special collections, opened an hour early one day and had their entire staff there to help. Librarians are a special breed of people.

So, the students got their projects ready, in all manner of conditions, and instead of holding a school competition, because, after all, it was just my classes, we had several other classes come in and critique the work. This wasn't about saying whether the project was good or bad, although some of that happened. This was about giving the students suggestions for improvement before we went to the district meet in March. I didn't have the slightest idea if these projects were genius, good, bad, or just plain ridiculous. I hadn't ever seen any NHD displays or presentations.

It soon became apparent that more important than the actual productions was the camaraderie that developed when other students came to assist. And, amen, NHD did not consider this cheating. In fact, NHD encouraged it. There was a novel idea—students helping other students. While NHD doesn't allow anyone other than the students to actually do the work, it lets others review the design and content of a project and give suggestions to any student in the competition. Think about that. What kind of leftist, communist program is this?

While the students were working on these projects, there was another change that year. The principal had decided that I would be the one to work with a student teacher from a local college's teacher-preparation program. I was ambivalent. More work? What would I do? What was my role? What would his job be? Would this be more babysitting? No idea. It turned out that Mr. Milios would be in charge in three of my classes; he would gradually take over the classes and be responsible for all the work, including preparing lessons, teaching, and grading.

He had a contagious energy and an infectious joy about life that he took with him everywhere he went. I really didn't care what he did; as long as he appeared every day and recharged us all, that would be enough. But there were these pesky requirements he had to meet, so he did prepare lessons, and organize and teach classes, and grade papers.

The students loved Mr. Milios. Well, at least all the young women loved Mr. Milios. His growing fan club appeared without fail at the end of every day at my classroom door. They were dressed to the nines; provocatively, one might say. Their makeup and hair was impeccable. They all looked like they were twenty-eight-years-old. They swooned and they swooned and they swooned.

"Is Mr. Milios hereeeee?" the lilting voices asked.
"Can we come in?"

Giggle, giggle, giggle.

And as they spotted him, they would exclaim, "Hiiiiiiiiiiiii, Mr. Milios!" in a chorus with emphasis on the drawn out, melodic, rhythmic "Hi." "How are youuuuuu today, Mr. Milios?"

Giggle, giggle, giggle.

And they weren't even my students. So Mr. Milios had a talk with these beautified groupies. Like a pro, maybe better than a pro, he conveyed to these weak-in-the-knees lovelies the need for teacher-student boundaries. I watched in awe.

We did have one problem. Jesse was an awkward, pimply, overweight sophomore young man in one of Mr. Milios' world-history classes. We needed the film-strip projector for one class and it was sitting at the back of the room all ready to go when Jesse walked across the row, banged into the projector's cart with such precision that the projector flew to the floor spitting out and breaking its lens and shocking its bulb into darkness. I didn't think I was being mean when I said, kiddingly, to Jesse, "Well, we know who won't be picking up any AV equipment for us from now on." The class laughed. Jesse laughed. The class moved on with a different plan. End of story.

Until parents' night a few weeks later. Since it was Mr. Milios' class, he would be doing the majority of talking to those parents. At one point, though, he disappeared. I walked out of the classroom looking for him and what I found was Jesse's mother pinning him to a locker. She was big; she was strong; she was determined; she was fierce. Her face showed no mercy. Her heavy arms went to each side of Mr. Milios whose back was up against the lockers. Her man-hands rested on the lockers. Mr. Milios was not escaping this conference; he also wasn't saying much. Mama was doing all the talking; something about Jesse's teacher humiliating Jesse in front of the whole class because a machine fell off its cart. I don't know what Mr. Milios said to her, but I do know he took the bullet for me. I never forgot that. I also don't know what Mr. Milios learned from this experience, but I do know what I learned: never mess with pimply, overweight, awkward, teen-age, young men. They come with very big mothers.

But I had also learned that I loved working with a student teacher. This was a good fit for me. I loved watching Mr. Milios come alive and progress. I loved watching the students respond. I loved seeing the interaction. I loved learning from Mr. Milios. I loved that I had way less work to do. And how could I have known that Mr. Milios was the first of hundreds of student teachers, including his cousin, a second Mr. Milios, with whom I would work?

In March we went to the district History-Day competition, full of confidence. It was a thirty-minute, joyful bus ride that Saturday to Oburn Middle School in Oburn, MA. The group was upbeat, singing and dancing in their seats, and high-fiving each other. This program was a lot of fun. When we arrived at the school, those with the table-tops set up their boards alongside those from other schools. Once everything was in place, we all started to look at the other entries. Our excitement would soon turn to something else. I went down the rows looking aghast at, and bowled over by, one phenomenal, professional-looking display after another. They weren't just aesthetically impeccable; the content showed university-level investigation. When I saw what other students had produced, I was mortified. Compared to the other projects, my students' boards looked like elementary work, poor elementary work, dumb elementary work.

I wanted to grab all the students' work and hightail it out of the building. At the very least, I wanted to hide and pretend I had nothing to do with these kids. Jack and Christine, who had worked together on their project on the Holy Roman Empire, picked up their boards which weren't really boards at all but pieces of cardboard (what did I know about all this, really?); stomped on them; ripped them to shreds; threw them in the wastebasket near the windows; and did run out of the building, crying. It was my fault; I had little understanding of the capabilities of high-school students. My pathetic expectations had been way too low, stupidly low, out-of-touch low, criminally low. I should have been arrested. I expected to be arrested. I was going to be arrested for causing emotional trauma to teenagers. Phenomenal headache.

The judges, one professional historian and three history professors, were not kind to my students, my children; how dare they hurt my children. They did, though, in the end, give lots of advice on how to make improvements for next year's program. It was no surprise when none of my students won anything. We were done with History Day for the year. The bus ride back was solemn. No one spoke, some slept, some just stared out the windows. Most of them had abruptly thrown their creations into the dumpster outside the school.

When we got back to class on the following Monday, I expected the students to be depressed, mad at me, mad at themselves, and feeling as if I had betrayed them and beaten them to a pulp with my incompetence.

*No! No! No!* That is not what happened. They were on fire. They couldn't sit still. They all wanted and tried to talk at once.

"Mrs. Page, Let us do it again next year," Mary pleaded.

"We know what to do now," Michelle claimed vehemently.

Kathleen cried, "You have to let us. Please, please, please."

"But, … you … won't … be … in … my … classes … next …

year," I responded very slowly, stretching out my words in disbelief. Was I hearing correctly?

"Then please let us help the students in next year's program," answered Curt.

"Or we will do it on our own," Clarice finished his sentence.

"Please, please, please. We all want to do it," Kara added.

"Blackstone could win," Bobby piped in.

"We know exactly how to help," Gloria promised.

Brad pushed his way into the conversation, "We know how to make everything way better."

You have to let us do this," Kathleen asserted again.

"Now we understand it," Ken explained.

I didn't know what "it" meant, but I knew I had another headache. Inconceivable headache. Intra-brain cacophony. Waves smashing. Blood rushing. Rocks crashing. Glass breaking. Ouch! More learning about adolescents, their resilience, their astounding abilities, their energy, and what factors might entice them to jump wholeheartedly into a learning stew.

Something big had happened. Had the academic devil won or lost the bet? What did it all mean?

## Chapter 15

## Tragedy, Triumph, and Adolescents

The next year at Blackstone was a banner year. The word had spread about the NHD program and suddenly there were students *wanting* to be in my world-history classes. My roster now included a third world-history class to accommodate the onslaught. That was fine with me because at the same time, that reduced my class load of U.S. history to one. A win, win. So that meant I would teach three world-history classes, one U.S. history class, and the sociology class.

In came the world-history students in three different classes, falling over each other, wanting only to know when they could start working on their History-Day projects.

"Mrs. Page," Jim said impatiently. "We know all about History Day. We want to get going right away."

"We are ready," Debbie chimed in.

"Are we going to start today?" Lori wanted to know.

I was flabbergasted and didn't waste a second. I invited all the History-Day graduates from the previous year, with all their stories of rejections and criticisms in tow, to come into my classes during their study periods. They didn't let me down. I stepped back and they took over the classes. What was I witnessing? What was I seeing? What was I learning? What were *they* learning? Here were high-school juniors, some of them on the football team—and we all know those noble-jock football players have no interest in learning—explaining how it all worked; what they, the new recruits, would have to do; how to select a topic or problem; how to do primary research; where to find things; what they should do first; what they should do next; how to put things in context;

how to show perspective; and when they, the History-Day graduates, would be back to assist.

That entire fall, in those three history classes, I did little more than help make connections among the chosen topics in the overall scheme of world history. The students, past and present, were doing all the work. Was there something special about learning from peers? Was there something special about working with technology? Was there something special about competition? What was going on? How did this all relate to what I saw at the Friday night football games?

In-between the work in the fall and the trip to the History-Day district competition in March, there was the special event we had all planned to watch on TV in my classroom. It was history in the making. It was January 28, 1986. Because it was in the middle of the lunch periods, there were hoards of students crossing the bridge from the cafeteria into the classroom building just as the event was about to begin. Students piled up at my door, like bees on honey, pleading with me to let them come in and stand at the back of the room to watch the show. Once again, they weren't even in my classes. Why did other teachers' students keep showing up at my door?

This was a monumental event. It was the launching of Space Shuttle Challenger and it would be the first time a member of the Teacher-in-Space Project, in this case social-studies teacher Christa McAuliffe from New Hampshire, would be on board. My room was jam packed, every seat filled, students squashed against each other on the sides and at the back of the room as we watched the countdown.

We didn't know that there was ice all over the launch pad. We didn't know that the Thiokol engineers who had devised the O-ring joints for the shuttle wanted NASA to postpone the launch. We didn't know it was too cold for the O-rings to work properly. We didn't know it was colder than minimum temperature permitted for the launch. We knew none of this. NASA opposed a delay and gave the okay for the launch to begin. It was incredibly exciting to be so present at such dramatic history. We all counted down, loudly and enthusiastically with the commentator:

10 ...

9 ...

8 ...

7...

6 ...

5 ...

4 ...

3 ...

2 ...

1 ...

*Lift Off!*

It was 11:38 a.m. EST. We were all shouting; we applauded and applauded. The Thiokol engineers were relieved as they watched Challenger separate from the launch pad. But seventy-three seconds after take-off, there was disaster beyond imagination. Space Shuttle Challenger broke apart and all of us stuffed in that room watched, glued to the TV, not exactly sure what we were seeing, not clear about what was happening. We tried to make sounds, but nothing came out. We stayed in place, motionless, with wide open mouths, looking like those dolls—the Byers Christmas Carolers. There I was, twenty-three years after standing in front of my class in Milltown hearing that President Kennedy had been shot, watching another titanic catastrophe. Just as twenty-three years earlier, I now stood in front of my students, looking this time at fifty, instead of thirty, teenagers who were staring back at me. I knew no more what to do this time than I had then. The rest of the day was a complete and utter blur.

The next day was very strange. I felt tired and sad and listless; the students were very quiet and distracted. We were all moving around as if in a slow-motion video. When we spoke at all, we were mumbling. We were all traumatized. The entire school had an eerie aura about it. During third period, Billy, who knew how shaken up I was over this horrific calamity, brought me a present he had been working on for quite some time in the shop class.

"Mrs. Page, I wasn't sure when to give this to you. I was going to save it for your birthday, but I decided to give it to you today. I made it in shop." The present was all wrapped up in blue tissue paper, the same powder-blue color as my sweater. "I hope you like it," Billy said sheepishly as he handed me the present. What a cute kid. What a sweet kid. Sometimes I loved my unexpected career.

My #2 necklace had become somewhat of a spirited joke with the students and a couple of them had given me different #2 charms as presents. Timmy had brought a charm back from a family vacation in Bermuda; Sharon had brought a silver and turquoise one from a Navajo reservation in Arizona. So, my first thought was that Billy had made me a new charm. But, no, this was too heavy and too big to be that. If I hung this thing, whatever it was, on my neck, I might choke to death.

I unwrapped the tissue paper carefully, feeling particularly appreciative and surprised that Billy would even think of me at all, but especially today after the Challenger tragedy. As I peeled away the layers of blue tissue paper, I saw that Billy had made the present out of wood. He had crafted it to precision. It was the nicest looking, true-to-scale, no-details-missing, ten-inch-wooden-perfect-penis that I had ever seen. Actually, it was the only wooden penis I had ever seen.

This wasn't funny. This was serious. I suppose I should have been intensely offended. I suppose I should have reprimanded Billy severely and immediately. I suppose I should have hauled Billy off to the principal's office. I suppose I should have called the guidance counselor to set up appointments with Billy before he did something dangerous or naughty with the real thing.

Instead of doing any of those things, as serious as this was, I burst out laughing. I flung myself around to face the front blackboard, penis in tow, to hide both it and my reaction from the class. The more I tried to swallow the laugh, the harder I laughed. *I. Could. Not. Stop. Laughing.* I was near choking. Tears started rolling down my cheeks. Get hold of yourself, I silently implored myself. Too much emotional overload. The anticipation of the Challenger launch, the dramatic lift off, the separating white clouds, and now a ten-inch-wooden-perfect-penis, wrapped in blue tissue paper, in my hand. Sometimes you just can't help it; you don't have control. You laugh and you laugh and you laugh.

What was the shop teacher thinking? That was my only question. Was he ever present in the room when his adolescent charges were building things? What else was under construction in that room across the bridge? A vagina? Breasts? Peruvian erotic statues in full bloom? It is true that teenagers don't always do appropriate things at appropriate times; not that there would ever be the right time to present your social-studies teacher with a ten-inch-perfectly-perfect-wooden-penis. Sometimes teenagers never do appropriate things at all, ever.

It was just a couple of weeks later when we had another

astonishing incident at Blackstone High School. I looked out my window and, beyond the driveway and parking lot, I could see the large green area. Blackstone was so very, beautifully green. The groundskeeper, wearing his protective, noise-cancelling headphones, was on his riding mower far in the distance. He was completely oblivious to the danger he was in. First I saw one flying arrow, then another, then another. And more. They kept coming. The thirty-inch aluminum missiles were flying all over the place, one after another, after another, all around the groundskeeper. The gym teacher was absent and there was a substitute teacher taking his place. And, for heaven's sake, the sub had gone ahead with their archery class and had apparently set the groundskeeper as the target. Before I even had time to call down to the office, one of the arrows flew over one of our buildings and landed in the roof of a car parked in front of that building. *Oh. My. God.*

Within minutes I heard the sirens and then saw the ambulance and fire engine coming up in front of the building. Mr. Leblanc and Mr. McCarthy were out there trying to attend to the person in the car who turned out to be a sixty-five-year-old man who, when the arrow hit, (totally true) had had a heart attack. The arrow didn't hit the man, but it was stuck in his car's roof. What could this poor man have been thinking? He was losing his mind? He was hallucinating? He was delusional? He had suddenly gone senile? The Lone Ranger and Tonto were riding through the premises? The Wampanoag Tribe had reappeared and wanted retribution for losing their land? The world was ending? He was in a movie? Luckily, he survived. And, thankfully, there were no more archery classes at Blackstone High School unless the regular gym teacher was present. Really, what was this crazy job all about? What more did I have to learn about adolescents?

111

We got to the History-Day district competition in March, this time with newly found understanding of the whole process, of the whole purpose, of the whole learning. The table-top projects held their own. The judges asked the students in-depth questions and scored them as follows: historical quality—including historical accuracy and content, reliability of primary sources, context, interpretation, and breadth and balance of research—(60%); significance of topic (20%); and clarity of presentation (20%). The exuberant project architects explained to the judges the relevance and background of their topics. They were combusting with energy and knowledge and analysis. And I was beaming. It was the same process with the synced slideshows, which were so good that one of them won first place. Maureen, Gayle, Shawn, and Bobby had created a masterful show about segregation and civil rights. It was brilliant. Apparently all my lesson plans—including those related to civil rights issues—that were born out of my headaches and brain disturbances were paying off.

With the slideshow project going to the state competition in May, now every student in every world-history class was offering ideas. At least a part of every class was spent debating ways to improve the project. All my history students were planning to go as spectators to the state competition and that one project became the core of their unity and cohesion, their *esprit de corps*. Maureen, Gayle, Shawn, and Bobby listened and made some complex and appropriate adjustments to their slideshow. Everyone had a stake in the outcome; everyone was invested.

We all piled on the buses that Saturday morning in April and set off for Caldwell High School in eastern Massachusetts where the state competition would take place. The Black-stone clan started to sing the two famous songs of the British rock band, Queen. First they swayed and seesawed to *We Will, We Will Rock You* and after several rousing rounds of that song, they broke into *We Are the Champions ...* . It was loud; it was very loud. The bus was throbbing and rocking and tipping. It was heavenly.

Students from all over the state arrived to demonstrate their competence and their topic mastery. And, holy mackerel, Maureen, Gayle, Shawn, and Bobby won third place. Blackstone students had gone from being embarrassed and pathetic underachievers to state winners in one year. Not too shabby. The Blackstone kids in the audience stomped and cheered and applauded and slapped each other for what seemed like forever. It was ridiculously, madly, freakingly, wickedly awesome. But, since only the first- and second-place state winners of History Day go on to the national competition, we would have to wait until next year for that trip. Nevertheless, we returned to the school as heroes.

I don't know which the students found more fascinating— the history they uncovered or the search, the treasure hunt with their peers, for that history. The students became so uninhibited and confident in their pursuits that they routinely found and contacted State and U.S. Representatives and Senators, CEOs, inventors, activists, scientists, history professors, veterans, labor officers, sports legends, writers, neighbors, anyone who had information. They searched through newspaper archives and special collections at the biggest and most famous libraries all over the country. And they even discovered important documents and artifacts in their own attics and also that their family members were often primary sources.

As if all that learning and winning were not enough, there was yet another event that raised my status with the students.

A couple of weeks after the state History-Day competition, we had a school assembly during fourth period. It was a rock-band concert. This was a very perspicacious rock band which was traveling the country making deals, with high schools, that went like this: if the school would let them use the auditorium Friday and Saturday nights for paid concerts, they, the band, would perform for free for a school assembly, and at the same time, they would deliver a strong anti-drug message to the students.

We all trouped across the bridge to the auditorium and sat in our assigned spaces and the concert began, my students much more excited than I. Not only did they get to skip a class, they got to listen to their kind of music. This was a seven-member band, dressed in comical, rag-tag costumes. They were wearing long, flapping coats over fluorescent-pink and fluorescent-green shirts and pants; and they were flashing jewelry everywhere—on their necks, on their fingers, in their ears, and up and down their arms. Their hair went in every direction and was of all lengths and colors. There was blue hair, green hair, orange hair, white hair, purple hair, yellow hair and shocking-pink hair.

And they were emphatically *loud*; so loud that I couldn't stay in the auditorium. Really, I just couldn't. My ears hurt a lot. If I stayed, certainly I would go deaf at an early age. I got up, abandoned my class, walked up the aisle of the auditorium and walked out the open back door, crossed the six-foot-wide, horizontal hallway along the back of the auditorium to stand at the wall at the far back of that hallway. I could still see my students and the band, but my ears weren't in pain back there. Soon, I had company. Almost all the other teachers deserted their students as well and they joined me in seeking refuge. There were a large bunch of us leaning against that wall.

All of a sudden, the band member with the orange hair jumped off the stage and raced at full speed up the aisle of the auditorium with his coat flying, flapping, and billowing. He darted out the back door, crossed the hallway, came right up to me, grabbed my hand, turned in the other direction, yanked me back into the auditorium, raced down the aisle at full clip with me in tow, flew up the stage steps, pranced into the middle of the band members who hadn't stopped playing, dropped my hand, reached behind one of the musicians, retrieved an instrument, slung it over my shoulder, and said, "Go." There I was, playing the guitar, jumping around following the band members' body cues, and singing along with this motley crew. The students went wild. I kept playing, jumping, and singing. Did I mention that I was faking it all?

"More, more, more!" the students kept yelling.

The concert ended, the students and I returned to the classroom. I stayed outside the door, not wanting to face these kids. I was monstrously embarrassed. I had made a complete fool of myself in front of four hundred and fifty students. I stood there and stood there, trying to get up the courage to go into the room; I was hoping the bell would ring telling the students to change classes. It didn't. Finally, I had to enter and when I did, it was with an intensely red face glowing like a fire. As I walked into the room, taking tiny, tiny steps, the class stood up and clapped.

"Mrs. Page, how long have you played the guitar?" asked Sandy.

"Mrs. Page, are you in a band?" John threw in his question.

"Mrs. Page, do you perform around here?" Collin wanted to know.

I couldn't disappoint.

"A long time."

"Yes."

"Not usually."

That last part was the only truth I spoke. I am a liar and a fraud. I made up words in Spanish at Milltown all those years ago; now I was telling these students I was a performing musician. I do sort of play the piano. Does that count? My stature with the students had gone from ho-hum-dull-mediocre-nothing-special teacher to superstar; superstar; super-duper-super superstar. Suddenly I owned it. I *was* a superstar, by goodness. But it wasn't fair. Male teachers could just talk about their cars with students and they were automatically megastars. I had to get on a stage with a bunch of bizarre-looking musicians and act like an idiot to have the same result. Perhaps we need another amendment to the Civil Rights Act, one that will make hero worship equal for male and female teachers. Where is Representative Howard Smith when you need him?

It was mostly a very productive year. We had made great strides in the U.S. history class with *The American Dream* book; we won third place at the History-Day state competition; I learned more than ever as I taught the sociology class; and I had discovered a whole lot more about adolescents, including how to make them worship me—that is, by making a nincompoop of myself and prevaricating.

There was more history in the making forty-five miles to the east. Just a month before that fortuitous state History-Day competition, and never far from my mind, the trial of *Anne Anderson et al. v. W.R. Grace & Co. et al.* had started at the federal courthouse in downtown Boston. It was a contentious trial that lasted seventy-eight days; a fairly young and inexperienced attorney was battling industrial giants. And one month after school had ended, in July, 1986, the jury ruled that W.R. Grace & Co. was responsible for polluting wells G and H in Woburn. The families received a few hundred thousand dollars apiece. At best this was inadequate compensation for their pain and suffering. It couldn't bring back their children. Grace settled for approximately eight million dollars without admitting to any wrongdoing. The jury dismissed the case against Beatrice for lack of evidence, although two years later, a three-judge panel for the U.S. Court of Appeals for the First Circuit ruled that Beatrice's lawyers had engaged in misconduct by withholding evidence. Unifirst had settled out of court for approximately one million dollars several months before the trial began. And still, it wasn't the end of the case. The EPA continued its investigation.

## Chapter 16

## Banned Books, Criminal Vacations, and Moving On

You guessed it. After that third-place finish at the state History-Day contest in the spring, even more students wanted to be in my world-history classes. In September of 1986, I would have four world-history classes and one U.S. history class. Once again, the History-Day graduates, and now we had two years of them, were going to come into our classes during their study periods and tutor the new, eager participants. The students chose their own groups, their own subjects, their own form of presentation, and began their quest.

There were many days I never left school until 5 p.m. My room was full of students wanting and needing to stay to work on their projects. Most days I would have to say, "You have to leave now; I have to go home."

"Mrs. Page, please just half an hour more, please."

"I can't, I'm sorry. I have to get home. You will have to leave."

"Ohhhh … whyyyyyy?"

It wasn't all happiness and good will, though. We did have some issues over group dynamics. One group of young women, in particular, were at each other like cats with sharp claws. Shelley came to me first.

"Mrs. Page, Julie and Debbie aren't doing what they are supposed to do. Sharon and I are doing all the work. We are getting very frustrated."

Then came Julie and Debbie to complain. "Mrs. Page, Shelly and Sharon aren't letting us do what we think we should on the project. We don't like their ideas and they are really bossy. Can we separate and do our own project? We would rather work on our own."

"*May* we separate and do our own project?" I corrected them. It was a teachable moment, wasn't it?

"May we separate and do our own project?" Julie repeated in the amended version.

"No, it's not possible." I already had almost twenty groups to monitor and guide. I couldn't handle one more group, one more topic, one more day after school. "I'm sorry."

So, the day after Julie and Debbie had complained to me, I sent them and their former friends and now arch enemies, Sharon and Shelley, into the hall—each with a chair, a notebook, and a pen. They were to sit at least three feet from each other, refrain from any kind of communication, and write down everything they liked about the work so far and everything they didn't like and why. Ten minutes later, I popped back into the hall and asked Debbie to sit with enemy Shelly, and Julie to sit with antagonist Sharon, and to share with each other everything they had written.

Another ten minutes later, I switched the pairs and they were to do the same thing with the new adversarial partner. A few more minutes and I sent them back to their individual places to write down at least five ways to solve the issues. And finally all four read their resolutions and solutions aloud to each other. Ten minutes left in the period and they came back into the room, explained the situation to the class, and detailed the new goals and new procedures they proposed to follow. The class then added their own two-cents worth of possible changes. Shelley, Sharon, Debbie, and Julie lived happily ever after in History-Day land. Job well done, Mrs. Page.

My U.S. history class was not nearly as much fun as my world-history classes, but it wasn't without its own personality and good times. During the Spring of 1987, there was the day when Shaun had forgotten his textbook. Forgetting books was nothing new to this class. Getting students, especially freshmen, to remember their pens and notebooks and books and homework is about as easy as getting molasses to flow uphill. It's probably a passive-aggressive thing. Or maybe these students had never needed to bring books and other school equipment to their classes at the junior high. That is the rule—always blame the previous teacher or school. It works well and is quite productive.

Parents and community members think that they, the parents, send their children off to school where teachers, whose salaries they pay, are actually teaching their ever-attentive sons and daughters. That is the fantasy. Let me put that rumor to rest right now. Teachers spend a whole lot of their time doing things like sending students to their lockers to retrieve all this forgotten stuff. First Johnny goes to his locker; when he returns, then Isabella goes to hers; and when she comes back, then Anthony goes—all holding up the start of the class. They always go to their lockers one-by-one because let's be real, three high-school students at their lockers at the same time would lead, for sure, to gargantuan misbehavior. There is no end to the trouble young people can get into at their lockers—laughing, talking, swearing, losing things, goofing around, kissing; you never know. You can't be too cautious.

This particular day, instead of delaying the class by sending Shaun to his locker, I asked him to push his desk over next to Carrie's and to share her book. Things were going fine until all of a sudden, my wide classroom door flew open with a terrific bang against the front blackboard. It scared us all. In barged big Mr. Carter. He ignored me completely, got as close as his bigness allowed to Shaun and roared at him, "Where is your book? Why didn't you bring it with you? Go get it and don't forget it again."

Here was this behemoth of a man standing over a five-foot, seated, freshman boy. Mr. Carter must have felt very powerful. Out he stormed, again as if I were invisible, slamming my door shut with another monstrous crash. He had rattled me, Shaun, and the entire class. Shaun had his book and I had a class in disarray. Thanks, Mr. Carter. That was very helpful.

Mr. Carter had been on one of his sprees. He had been roaming the halls, staring like a private investigator, with his bug-eyes, into every classroom, and repeating a version of the scene with Shaun wherever he saw something amiss. It finally came to me that maybe Mr. Carter had OCD, what with his repeated checking, his fixation on his pennies, his heightened and intense attention to detail, his micromanagement of everyone and everything. It's a wonder with these controlling administrative characters that any meaningful teaching and learning ever occurs.

March of 1987 was a busy month. As expected, students were getting into fights in and out of school. An uptick in student combat is always the first clue that spring has arrived; it happens every year like clockwork. I remembered the fight the previous year when sophomore girls, Brittany and Melissa, attacked each other on the bridge. They had gotten too wild and had thrown each other through the plate-glass wall and had landed on the driveway below. They recovered from their injuries after some time in the hospital, but I was hoping that a battle like that wouldn't happen this year. Teenage young women can be vicious.

There was something else that happened right on cue every spring. As expected, students were heading to Disney World on their unauthorized vacations with their families. Came the day that Mary Jane appeared at my desk with a note from her mother.

> *Mrs. Page,*
> *Please give Mary Jane assignments for the next two weeks. Our family will be in Florida on vacation.*
> *Thank you, Doreen Cain*

This was the tenth student to bring me such a note in the past two weeks. Blackstone High School was the only school where I had experienced these *special* vacations at any random time of the year. Now, it might not be a problem for elementary teachers who have twenty students total. Maybe it is, I don't know. But when you have one hundred and fifty students and you receive ten of these notes requesting that you take your own time to write down all the assignments, none of which you have even thought about yet, let alone jotted down anywhere, that adds up to a whole lot of your time. That is just one problem. Another is that in the three years I had been teaching at Blackstone, not one student who had requested and received assignments for a vacation had ever done them. *Not one.* All that time and effort wasted.

Additionally, things move very quickly at the high school, especially in a history class where you can only hope you will reach World War II or the Vietnam War (as if those markers note when the history of the world ended) by the end of the year. For that and other reasons, including administratively-determined disruptions like snow days, assemblies, and student-release days, no good teacher can stick to a set plan for two weeks in advance. Too many things happen for a teacher not to change something in that time period, so whatever you give to the vacation-planning student, who isn't going to do it anyway, is, in the end, irrelevant. And when the student returns, always minus completed assignments, you have to stay after school with that student to administer missed tests and issue the real homework.

One more thing, while I am on this soap box. You know I am on a soap box, right? Massachusetts law states that it is a crime to induce, or attempt to induce, a minor to miss school, and it is clear that schools and parents pay no attention to this in relation to vacations. I hadn't had an office-invitational in quite a while. It was time. It would be my sixth.

"Mary Jane, I am sorry. I am not going to do that. Please tell your mother she may call me if she wants to talk to me."

The next day, there it was in my mailbox, just as I knew it would be: *See me immediately!* You could always tell when Vice Principal McCarthy was angry. He never signed his name when he was urgently mad; but his handwriting was unmistakable.

The meeting. This mild-mannered ex-seminarian was really, really mad. I had never seen him raise his voice, but he did now. "What do you mean, you aren't going to give Mary Jane the assignments? Yes, you will."

Oh, boy, Mrs. Cain must have chewed him out.

"No, I am not going to! I am not going to!" I adamantly fumed twice just to make sure he heard me. I explained my arguments and threw in the *truant* word. That really sent him over the edge. There was quite a conversation that ensued.

"I am not going to take my time to do that. I have never had even one student do any of the work I have given them for their *illegitimate* school vacations. Let them go on vacation; I don't care, but I am not going to spend my time preparing individual assignments for Mary Jane or anyone else who decides to go on vacation at any old time."

I was just as mad; I was really fed up with it all. And besides, why should they get to go on vacation when I couldn't?

I didn't say that last part to Mr. McCarthy.

"Mrs. Cain wants her daughter to keep up with the class; she needs the assignments. You have to prepare them for her."

"If she wants her daughter to keep up with the class, she needs to not be going to Disney World during school time. We get vacations in February and April. That is what they are for. No, I don't have to prepare them. It is a crime to induce a minor to miss school." I snuck in the big guns. I was really over the top.

"All the other teachers do this for their students. You need to give her the assignments," Mr. McCarthy argued in his now monotone voice. I think he was trying to de-escalate my intensity.

"No, I am not going to," I kept it up. "If you want her to have assignments, you will have to invent some for her yourself, because I am not going to do it."

And with that, I got up and walked out of the office.

Oh boy, what had I done? Stood my ground, for one thing. Probably gotten myself fired for another. No, wait. The law was on my side. These willy-nilly vacations were ridiculous. Why were we condoning them? We shouldn't be in the business of encouraging these school-time vacations. I had never had to contend with this at any other school. Why were these parents running amuck with their vacations at Blackstone High School. Is this what the *entitled* folks do? I didn't know.

Two days later, the principal called an emergency, after-school meeting to clarify policy on giving students homework for private vacations. I knew the teachers weren't going to go down McCarthy or LeBlanc Lane. This was a prickly burr in all our sides.

End of meeting score: Mrs. Page = 1; Mr. McCarthy and Mr.

Leblanc = 0.

I admit it. This story might not be totally accurate. This might not be quite how it played out, but if it didn't play out exactly this way, it should have.

It was soon time to order books for the next academic year. Although I now had only one U.S. history class, there would be more U.S. history classes for the other social-studies teachers next year to accommodate the big class of eighth graders coming up from the junior-high school. I called Ginny, the sales representative at Scott, Foresman, & Co., to order twenty-five more of *The American Dream* books, only to be told that Scott, Foresman, & Co. was going to stop publishing that book.

"*Why*? *Why*? *Why*?" I shrieked. I don't know if I was stunned, in a panic, furious, confused, or all of the above.

"Because Alabama has banned the book, so it won't be worthwhile for us to publish it anymore," she answered.

"They banned the book? Why did they ban the book?" I was *loud.*

"Because it requires that students think for themselves."

I was speechless. There was nothing I could say. There is still nothing I can say, because the idea of not wanting students to think for themselves is just too extraordinary, too ludicrous, too preposterous, too nonsensical for me to grasp.

In what came to be called the *Alabama Textbook Case*, more than six hundred parents and teachers had brought suit, Smith v. Board of School Commissioners, in regard to many textbooks they believed promoted a certain religious, or perhaps more accurately an anti-religious, belief called *secular humanism.* They defined secular humanism as the belief that people should solve their own problems without the aid of God; and they blamed this form of religion, as they saw it, on the philosophy of John Dewey who was arguably the most influential educational reformer of the twentieth century. These plaintiffs claimed the books were hostile to the beliefs of many Christians and lacked a biblically-based framework for decision- and conclusion-making. And since these books, in their view, promoted a religion—secular humanism—as such, they violated the separation of church-vs.-state tenet of the United States Constitution.

U.S. District Court Judge W. Brevard Hand of Mobile, Alabama, who ruled on the case, agreed with the plaintiffs and posited that there *was* secular humanism and a hyper-relativism in American curriculum, such as when students were required to look at, investigate, and analyze different materials and come to their own conclusions. Accordingly, he banned forty-four books in his decision on March 4, 1987, basing much of his decision on the testimony of Russell Kirk—political theorist, historian, and standard bearer of traditional conservatism—who traced the origin of secular humanism not only to John Dewey but also to Marxist theory. My brain wanted to blow up.

Thirty-nine of those books were history or social-studies books, one of which was my treasured *The American Dream*. Five of the books were home economics books. Scott, Foresman, & Co. were swift and sure. They stopped publishing the book immediately. For them it was all about the money they would lose if they lost Alabama, and probably Texas at the same time, as customers. I don't think, even twenty-five years later, I have recovered from what I considered the uninformed, no, the whacky, theory of Judge Hand, Russell Kirk, and those hundreds of parents. And still, today, political and religious powers control or strongly influence textbook adoption in twenty-one states. I admit it; my bias is showing.

Unfortunately, it was too late to help me with book ordering or to head off the decision by Scott, Foresman, & Co. when, five months later, on August, 26, 1987, Judge Frank Johnson, Jr. of the 11th District U.S. Court of Appeals in Alabama, reversed Judge Hand's decision. Kudos to you, Judge Johnson.

Once again, we were heading to the NHD contests. And once again the History-Day graduates at Blackstone came to our classes to assist. Now there were four world-history classes involved in the program. I needed all the help I could get. The Blackstone entries sailed past the district match-up, with lots of winners. And there we were on the way to the state competition. Not only did the district winners go, but many of their fellow contestants who hadn't placed, but wanted to support the winners, went along. And also there were the History-Day graduates from the previous years. Some came on the buses; some drove their own cars. We were a History-Day caravan.

The clamor, the jumping, the dancing, and the crying that occurred when Jason, Tommy, Karl, and Mike won second prize for their table-top project on Prohibition was sublime. And what was maybe lost on most of them was the amazing and unheard of back story that these four young men were on the Blackstone tennis team which was, at the exact same time as the state HD contest, in the state tennis finals. They had had a difficult decision to make—whether to go to History Day or to join their tennis teammates. Noble jocks had decided to leave the athletic fiefdom. I think there were fireworks all over the United States the day these four young men chose History Day. Academics over athletics. What a concept. Would that mean they couldn't go back to the fiefdom? Did this mean certain blackballing?

About a week prior to the day of competition, I had had a visit from Coach Dillon. He was not happy with me or these four young men who were his tennis-team members and whom he pretty much considered his, period. He didn't, wouldn't believe that I had had nothing to do with their decision to skip the tennis state championships. I had probably threatened them with their grades or something equally sinister, he accused. Not so. It was their decision. Couch Dillon wanted me to convince them to change their minds. Ha! Hell would freeze over and the cows would have to come home first.

"It better not happen next year," he had warned me gruffly, and with that, he had flown out of the room, his face all puffed up and bluish-red with veins popping out everywhere.

Coach Dillon wasn't the only person mad at me. A few days before *he* had appeared at my door, Mrs. Watson, the English-literature teacher, had had a friendly chat with me about our common students spending too much time on History-Day work and not having enough time to do their English assignments. And next it was the math teacher, Miss Kaplan, who had come with the same beef. And eventually I got my seventh office-invitational. Principal LeBlanc wanted to know what was going on that there were teachers complaining to him about this program and its impact on their students' attention in their classes and to their work. How could I respond to indictments about students spending too much time on History Day, especially when these students were the ones asking me to stay after school so they could do it. I was speechless, truly speechless. I just raised both my arms and shrugged. My whole face was squinched in incredulity.

Although the Blackstone students didn't win at the national competition at the University of Maryland, I doubt they will forget the trip or that their project became a traveling museum exhibit in the state of Massachusetts for the next year.

And, if you look in the 1987 yearbook of Blackstone High School, you will see that others remember their NHD experiences also. There you will find, under many graduates' photos, the listing of NHD as the *most memorable event* of their high school years. The graduates of the past NHD programs were actually graduating from high school.

And in a way, I was also. I had decided to take a year's leave of absence to begin a doctoral program. I really did want to figure out what had been going on in these last three and a half years to lead to what I had observed. Especially after the first year, why had students been so eager to do so much work? Why hadn't they resisted the process? Why had they invested so much time? How had they become so proficient in conducting research? Why had students chosen this program over a sport's state finals? Why didn't students get this involved in traditional school work?

In other words, what drew the students to the NHD program? I asked myself the questions I had asked before and added some new ones: Was it the competition? Was it the camaraderie? Peer assistance? The use of technology? The history treasure hunt? The discoveries? What was driving the students? And how did their learning through the NHD process differ from any other kind of learning? Was it more substantial, more in-depth? Was it longer lasting? How was it different, if at all, from the kind of learning the students had experienced in the law class when they had put me on trial? What meaning was there in all of this for the students?

Maybe I could figure this all out, create an academic potion, sell it, and get rich. And then, maybe, my brain could stop tangling itself up and get some rest.

## Chapter 17

## A Medical Emergency

A year passed, a year of study at the University of Massachusetts. And on September 6, 1988, the day before the new public-school year would begin, with my brain stuffed with all kinds of new theories and ideas, I drove up the driveway to Blackstone High School to reclaim my teaching position. About halfway up the driveway, something happened akin to what had happened when I had assigned that program about the Vikings at Norwalk Junior High School. My mouth got desert dry. I was dizzy, very, very dizzy. I think I was having a stroke. My arms went limp. I tried to talk to myself and couldn't make any sounds. My face felt funny on one side; I was definitely having a stroke. Maybe it was a heart attack. There was pain in my chest and in my jaw. There was pain in my shoulder. Yes, it was a heart attack. As if by wishing it so, I got the car into a parking space, sort of rolled out of the door, and somehow got to the principal's office, surprising myself that I hadn't dropped dead on the way.

The principal knew something was wrong just by looking at me. He jumped to his feet and helped me into a chair. I spoke, but I didn't know who was speaking. Was I saying that? "Mr. LeBlanc, I can't do this. I can't come back. I need to return to the program at UMass." Suddenly, and as quickly as I had spoken, the stroke symptoms disappeared. I was able to stand, I was even smiling. The pain left my chest. I took a very deep breath. I could feel the color returning to my face. I hadn't had a heart attack or a stroke.

Mr. Leblanc replied, "Marilyn, it's fine. You need to do what you need to do." I doubt he would have been quite so generous if Mr. Pinaro, the man who had been my replacement for my sabbatical year, and who is now Blackstone's principal, hadn't been waiting in the wings for my job.

Most likely Mr. LeBlanc breathed his own sigh of relief that he wouldn't have to deal again with me, with the National History Day program, with students staying too late after school, with providing buses to district competitions, with paying for winners' trips to Maryland, with students choosing NHD over critical sports teams, or with the other teachers complaining that History Day was causing their students' inattentiveness; not to mention not having to deal with parents angered over my unwillingness to write out assignments for their children's criminal vacations. All those pesky nuisances that get in the way of running a tight ship. No wonder he said, "Marilyn, it's fine."

I practically skipped to my car with a lightness I hadn't felt probably since 1963 when I had signed onto this unintentional profession. I deposited all the work, all the investment of time and emotion, and all the aggravations somewhere deep in an untouchable part of my brain bank. My public school teaching had come to its soundless, albeit nearly fatal, end. No fireworks exploded; no brass band played; there was no going-away party; and no one other than Mr. LeBlanc had a chance to say goodbye.

# PART III

## *THE NEXT ACT*

## Chapter 18

## Student Teachers, Flashback, and Those Damn Diagrams Labels

Money. There is never enough. This would have been my chance to jump off this adventitious education ship or train or whatever it was. There were still times when I wondered what I was doing in this line of work. And right now, I still had time to become a director of some phenomenal, altruistic company that would help save people in third-world countries as I had originally wanted to do; better yet, I could help save people in our own country. Or, I could become a famous attorney, maybe a malpractice attorney or a family attorney. No, wait, an immigration attorney; that's where the action would be. The Immigration Reform and Control Act of 1986, offering citizenship to illegals who had been in the United States since 1982, but forcing others—including war refugees—to return to their home countries, was a hot coal jolting thousands of people. Definitely, that's where the action would be. Or, maybe I could become a quantum physicist, but first I would have to figure out what it is a quantum physicist does and with what and to whom.

Money. There wasn't any. For any of these pursuits I would need further study and that meant money, lots of money. The five-year-old I had put on the bus on that first day of forced busing in Boston back in 1974, was entering college. And his siblings were coming up right behind him. There was one thing I didn't need money for and that was a doctoral program in education. Not only would the university waive my tuition, but it would pay me a stipend to supervise student teachers all over eastern Massachusetts. Sometimes you just have to take the choice that is available, whether it's exactly what you want to do or not. Or, maybe this was all just rationalizing. Wimpiness and the path of least resistance had most likely taken over. Regardless of why, I stayed on the train and just switched tracks.

On the new, university course, in five years of supervising these student teachers and interns, I was in over two hundred schools. There were scary schools, stagnant schools, lively schools, dynamo schools, monstrous schools, small schools, urban schools, suburban schools, mediocre schools, menacing schools, progressive schools, safe schools, negative schools, schools I wanted to be in, and schools I wanted to get the heck out of. As for principals and vice principals, I met them all—friendly, hostile, skillful, dim-witted, charismatic, frightened, with-it, not-with-it, controlling, cooperative, uncooperative, condescending, dismissive, funny, boring, empowering, all kinds of them. None were as professional as Mr. LeBlanc or Mr. McCarthy. These two men had set the bar. Regardless of our disagreements, they were a class act—always putting the students first. And even though Mr. LeBlanc was at heart a noble jock, he always did what was right academically. Nice job, Mr. Leblanc and Mr. McCarthy. I liked you both a whole lot.

There was American High School, which at that time was across the street from the famous, academically-challenging Boston Latin School—the oldest public school in the nation. Although in a relatively safe area of Boston, American High had thick, heavy chains on every door except for the door which was the only way in and the only way out. Once school began in the morning, the security guard closed and locked this entry-exit door as well. He sealed up the students and teachers inside as if they had stepped into a super-sized freezer bag and he had zippered it shut. I had to punch in a special code to enter. It might as well have been a speakeasy, a freezer-bag speakeasy.

Once I got inside, a four-story escalator was staring me in the face. Never mind a speakeasy, I thought I was at Macy's. I rode up to the third floor expecting to see the signs announcing: *Women's Dresses; Children's Clothing; Women's Shoes.* I think I moved off the escalator just by the sheer force of the student mass behind me. I found the room James was in and I sat in the back waiting for the office's morning announcements to finish.

> *Don't forget there will be drama club rehearsals this afternoon at 2:30 p.m. And we welcome back Tylissa Mason from her maternity leave. Everyone, have a productive day.*

That was pretty nice, the principal acknowledging that one of the teachers had returned after having a baby. Okay, so it wasn't a teacher; it was a fourteen-year-old freshman girl. I had so much to learn about inner-city schools.

After I had observed and videotaped James teaching, and after we had reviewed the videotape, he and I rode the escalator down together so we could continue to discuss his lesson as I was leaving for another appointment.

I commented, "You are very lucky to have a class with only thirteen students. You will be able to do so much and will get to know them all really well."

"Mrs. Page," James corrected me, "there were thirteen students in my class today; I have thirteen students every day, but they are always a different thirteen. There are really thirty-nine students in the class, but this is all that ever show up. Have you got any ideas on how to handle this?"

"Not even one," I admitted, stunned. I wanted to yell a few expletives, but didn't. I had no idea how to advise James.

My next stop that day was the Boston Vocational Technical School. It was huge, but it didn't have an escalator like American High School did. Yet, the inside cavity of the school was so massive that every year students built a whole darn house in there. Robert, the student teacher, was a genius with his eleventh-grade English class which was a three-way split-population of Latino, Asian, and black students. Most of the whites, remember, had fled the city in the mandated busing mess or were now in private or parochial school.

On this day, Terrell first and then DeShawn showed the class excerpts they had read from Salinger's *Catcher in the Rye*. Each, as instructed, had put the selection on a transparency for the overhead projector, and each, in turn, explained what meaning the selection had for him. Terrell had chosen a segment about the main character Holden meeting with his former friend Sally and trying to convince her to run away with him to Vermont or Massachusetts. DeShawn's excerpt was much heavier. It was the description of Holden seeking refuge at the apartment of his former English teacher, Mr. Antolini, and waking up to find Mr. Antolini stroking his head.

I didn't have to worry about Robert. He managed both presentations and subsequent discussions with the sensitivity and control appropriate for a class of sixteen-year-olds. He was a natural with the content and with the students, and he was doing a far better job than I could have. His greatest feat in my mind was that he had gotten these students, both of whom were living in their cars, to read a book at all.

My concerns weren't with Robert. They were with getting out of the school safely; with finding my car still intact in the parking lot; and with making it back over Mission Hill without being on the wrong end of one of the daytime drive-by shootings that were happening more and more frequently. I managed it all and drove as fast as I could down Huntington Ave. Sometimes just getting into and out of an inner-city school is half the battle.

It was in February, 1990, when I headed for the Hurncoat Street Middle School in Worcester. This was my town. I had grown up here. I had gone to school here. I knew every street in the city. Hurncoat Street Middle School, previously known as Hurncoat Street Junior High School, had long had the reputation as one of the best schools in the city. When I approached the front door, I could see things had changed. Taped to the glass was a big sign that read: *Anyone Found Carrying a Gun to School Will Be Suspended for One Week.* A gun? One week? A middle school? How can a city change so fast and so dramatically? Oh, hold on, the last time I had been anywhere near there was thirty-five years before.

Inside, the school was practically on lockdown. I had to sign in and get a big temporary badge to wear for all to see. Only two lavs, one girls' lav and one boys' lav, were open during the day so as to prevent the usual, or, here, maybe the unusual, lavatory high jinks. A teacher, fulfilling contractual duties, sat outside each of the open lavs. Students had to sign into and out of the lav with that teacher, and when another student was already in the lav, even though there were six stalls, others had to wait outside in plain view of the teacher, until that other person came out. The school had removed all of the stall doors to prevent hidden bad behavior in there. The students also had to carry an oversized pass with them to and from the lav. This Herculean pass was in the form of an eighteen-inch wooden key. It might as well have been a big wooden cross.

I found Lanie in her classroom teaching seventh-grade math. I marveled at her ability to deal with so many students, at least thirty, half of whom barely spoke English. I was learning a lot in Inner-City 101. I learned for sure, that inner-city teaching in 1990 was no walk in the park and couldn't be compared to teaching in Blackstone or Norwalk or Milltown or King Metacomet or Woburn or even to my inner-city experience in Gary, Indiana, twenty-five years earlier. Lanie earned an A just for showing up and surviving.

I finished the visit with Lanie, and, as if by internal radar, I headed down Hurncoat Street, merged onto Lincoln, moved onto Main Street, and drove into and through the now practically deserted downtown Worcester. This had been the bustling hub of my growing-up years. All the big and important stores had been there: Denholm's, where I would stand and wait for the bus that finally went up Heard-Street hill; Barnard's, where my great aunt worked selling coats; Woolworth's, where I had worked and had bought the hamster without my parents' permission and which I had had to keep in the cellar only to find him icy-cold and dead one morning; Lerner's, on the corner of Main and Pleasant, where you could find an inexpensive outfit; Marcus', where I had spent my senior year in high school working every afternoon carrying wedding gowns out of the storeroom for brides-to-be, taking the gowns out of the bags, waiting for the brides to try them on, then packing them back into their clear-plastic covers, and hauling them back to the storeroom; the Nature Food Store that Grandma Beckford managed and in which she worked until she was seventy-five-years old; Sherer's; Grant's; Newberry's; Kresge's; and Clayton's. There, across from Denholm's, was the still-functioning Worcester City Hall, where Grandma Beckford had conducted her sit-in all those years ago. I continued on Main Street past St. Peter's High School, then past Clark University on the right, past Crystal

Park on the left, and then I turned left onto Freeland Street; and there it was— South Middle School. Formerly this had been South High School and I was one of her graduates. It was here that I had been the invincible academic queen of my little kingdom. It was here that my friend Allan had made me laugh every day of my senior year. It was here that I had learned how, and how much fun it was, to skip school.

This was an old building, old enough that Dad had also graduated from this high school. But it was just as stately, just as majestic, just as welcoming, just as classic as it had been thirty-five years before. I checked in at the office, and Mr. Martinez, the principal, understanding my history with the building, gave me free reign to go where I wanted. I checked out every room in the building. It appeared that virtually nothing had changed since I had roamed the halls. The auditorium, the cafeteria, the gym, the library, all seemed the same. I was transported back to the bustling halls of my carefree teenage years.

There, on the second floor, in the front corner, was Mr. Storen's room. We all had wanted to be in his class, mainly because we all thought he was insane and all we did was laugh in there. Every day in Mr. Storen's class was like watching one of Shakespeare's comedies, or maybe more like being in one. The room looked exactly the same. The big windows, two on the front, two on the side, with their dark, wood trim, were still there. I could feel Mr. Storen's ghost roaming up and down the aisles and I could see all of us snickering and chuckling as he passed our desks. I didn't see the twelve-year-olds sitting at those desks now.

I headed down the stairs to the back of the building and towards Mr. Carding's room. And as I came around the corner, there was Allan coming around a different corner, half running towards me. He was always in a hurry and here he was skillfully swerving around the twelve- and thirteen-year-olds who now bumped and tripped through our halls. And there *it* was, that smile that lit up South High School. And just as he did then, Allan, whom everyone but me called Skip, was making me laugh out loud again. He was seventeen and I was sixteen and we were making our way through and past our old friends, the fourteen- to eighteen-year-olds who knew how to walk, on our way to Room 10.

Every day in Mr. Carding's room, Allan and I played a game while Mr. Carding was trying his best to teach us English grammar. I sat in the third seat from the front up against the side blackboard, and Allan sat right behind me. Mr. Carding was a very nice man and a very boring teacher. Our endeavor involved counting how many times he would say "um" in a class period. Allan and I had different ways of tracking each "um," but at the end of class we always compared notes.

"How many did you get?" I would ask.

"I got three hundred and one," he would say.

"No, you missed some; it was more like four hundred and ninety-five," I would counter.

It was hundreds of times. It seemed like thousands. Our method for staying awake was counting what was putting us to sleep. We had figured it out that during our senior year, Mr. Carding had said "um" approximately seventy-five thousand, two hundred and ninety times. To this very day, I can feel my teeth grinding viciously every time I hear an "um."

And there was Mr. Tride's room and his biology and botany labs, no-nonsense places for serious scientific study and students. All the brains, all the would-be doctors, biologists, botanists, and environmentalists were in there before, during, and after school whenever they could, always talking about things like cells and anatomy and bugs and specimens and stamens and pistils and other unpleasant things like that. They loved hanging out with Mr. Tride. His protégé, and my childhood and high-school friend, Eddy Schofield, would turn out to be the person who, while I was busy supervising student teachers, would lead others to establish the Thoreau County Conservation Alliance to save Walden Woods from commercial development. Mr. Tride would have been proud.

The chemistry lab was a more relaxed scientific environment. Good memories came flooding back. Cute Mr. Benjamin Gernstein, or Benny as we liked to call him, was one of South High's favorite teachers. He was always teaching us how to be safe and why we should want to understand all the periodic tables of chemical elements. Everyone respected Mr. Gernstein. So when he said, "Get your goggles on; get your apron on; put your gloves on," we did. And when he reminded us, "No running, no joking, no fooling around," we tried to comply. But there was that one day when Roger wasn't paying attention when he bent over his Bunsen burner and he set himself on fire. It took awhile for his eyebrows to grow back. High school was fun, a lot of fun. I was in a time warp.

I was there in my old high school to observe Darren teach his eighth-grade English class. I gave him the highest possible grade, not because I paid any attention to what he was doing, but because I didn't. I completely ignored his lesson; I am sorry to say I neglected him. I didn't, couldn't even see him. He was in Room 5 and all I could see was Mr. Neelson smacking his five-foot-long pointer-stick on the desks.

Mr. Neelson, a physical giant of a man, had an interesting approach to teaching U.S. history. We had to memorize the entire reading assignment each night and the next day he would call on us individually to recite verbatim a random paragraph.

"Marilyn, your turn," Mr. Neelson would announce. I would stand up next to my desk as he required that we all do when performing, and would say something like this from my *American Dream* book, but from a much older text:

> *In Boston, British troops roamed the city, ever watchful of the ragged colonial army posted at the city's edge. In Quebec, General Richard Montgomery had been killed by British troops this very day, and also dead was the rebel plan of taking British Canada. King George III had recently declared that the colonies were in open rebellion and that he was planning to take drastic steps. Indeed, just a week previous, a royal proclamation had closed the colonies to all trade. But France had sent word that it viewed the colonial cause as a chance to seek revenge on its hated enemy, Britain.*

Any incorrect word and *crack* went the pointer on a desk. Everyone would jump out of a half-sleep. Wouldn't it have been entertaining to use Victor Borge's *Phonetic Punctuation* routine, using onomatopoeic sounds, to enhance the whole show and the listeners' enjoyment? I don't know what kept me from delivering on that impulse.

It wasn't just Mr. Neelson's odd teaching method; I didn't understand his version of the American Revolution. (For some reason, this high school taught the entire U.S. history.) I had just returned from living in England with my family. Dad's company had transferred him to a plant twenty miles outside of London and I had attended the secondary school there for what would have been my junior year in high school. So I had already learned about the American War of Independence, as the Brits called it, while I was in England. Mr. Shaver, at the Garden City Secondary School, had told a totally different account of that war. Is it any wonder, given Mr. Neelson's stick-whacking and his arbitrary account of the

American Revolution, that I was ambivalent about U.S. history, let alone teaching it.

I felt really bad about Miss Hamlett, the French teacher. I did go into what had been her classroom and looked around and I did remember what had happened in there. I had a pit in my stomach. It hadn't been my proudest moment. I was a sophomore. Miss Hamlett was a very kind, big woman, and she was blind. It came to me one foolish day that it would be really funny to move her chair so that when she walked in and went to sit down, she would fall on the floor. That would be priceless, wouldn't it? I didn't just move the chair; I tied it to the cord of the window shade and hung it out the window at the far side of her classroom.

Miss Hamlett entered the room and said, "*Bonjour!*" and walked carefully towards her desk and chair. She didn't fall, though, because her hands couldn't feel or find the chair, so she didn't try to sit. She was much smarter than I was.

She asked (in English), "Where is my chair? Who took my chair?" Her voice was shaking.

Miss Hamlett had to have a student helper in each of her classes and in this particular class that was I. Just when you thought it couldn't get any worse. I was her assistant; I had hung the chair out the window.

"Marilyn, where is my chair? Who moved it?" she repeated, her anxiety growing.

"I will get it for you," I quickly responded. "I know where it is, but I don't know who put it there."

The whole class was guffawing. The students had their hands over their mouths as they tried to stifle louder laughter. It was awful; it was evil; it was depraved. It was a despicable thing to do. What possessed me to do it? Who knows. What possesses teenagers to do the things they do—to get reactions, to have fun, wanting to be popular, to prove something, or maybe, for the same reasons many people climb mountains, just because they can. Yes, teenagers do the darnedest, silliest, most ridiculous things anyone can imagine, like stealing a blind teacher's chair and hanging it out the window; shooting thirty-inch aluminum arrows at an oblivious groundskeeper riding his lawnmower; spreading feces all over a lavatory, all over two lavatories; tossing and shutting peers in lockers; hanging dead chickens on the school's doors; spray-painting geometric patterns in black and white on teachers' cars; whittling the perfectly-perfect-wooden-penis in shop class. The list is never-ending. We can probably blame it all on cognitive incongruity. Hitch the growing ability to think abstractly—and all the new and conflicting ideas that generates—with the ever present need of a teen or pre-teen to figure out who he is, *et voilà*: odd, irrational, nutty, and out-of-character behavior. I think of it as the brain getting overloaded and overworked and then short-circuiting. Boing! Boing!

But teenagers are ultra-loyal just as my own son was when he took the blame for his friend who had thrown a drum lid at the smoke detector in the high-school band room and had set off the fire alarm that called firemen and equipment from the school's three towns. The school fined us eight hundred and fifty dollars for being parents to a false, false-alarm ringer. He would rather have gone to Guantanamo Bay and undergone water boarding than to snitch on his friend.

The whole school knew what had happened in Miss Hamlett's class. No one ever tattled on me. And apparently I was too much of a wus to come clean. I still feel bad.

*Dear Miss Hamlett,*
*I did it and I am soooooo sorry. I feel terrible. I was an*

145

*idiot. Please forgive me.*
*Your faithful assistant, Marilyn*

Most of the student teachers I supervised during those five years became teachers; maybe one even became a teacher-of-the-year.  There were some, though, who didn't make it.  There was Nicolas who showed up at Hennington High School every day in his sweat suit.  He would sit at the back of his room while student after student read out loud, from a newspaper, some *current event*, that wasn't really a current event.  He would be in his self-induced coma, and unattended mayhem would break loose all around.  There was Ted at Cannon High School who found the students' disrespect and lack of attention more than he had bargained for and who quit halfway through the practicum.  He never figured out how to pull off the give and take necessary with teenagers.

I thought Elizabeth would make it, but that day that some of her students went wild and pretty much destroyed her classroom, I knew that it was all over.  Her choice.  And there was Jeff.  Arrogant, handsome Jeff.  His principal at Norell High School found him having sex with one of his students in the teachers' meeting room.  Did he not quite understand the concept of teacher-student conference?

Kaitlin did everything right.  She was prepared; she was keen; she was organized; she was quick; she was respected; she was beautiful.  She was teaching English to three classes at Dorwood High School and one of those classes was a senior English-literature class. It was a lopsided group with twenty young men and three young women.  If you know anything about seniors and about seniors in April and May, you know they have already checked out mentally.  They are just counting the days; they just take up space.  They are done.

I was making the last visit to Kaitlin before her practicum

would end. It was April. The class was reading *Macbeth* and on this particular day Kaitlin decided to teach the students how to diagram the plot of a story. This wasn't anything new. Aristotle had used this kind of diagram in teaching about drama and he had defined three simple parts of a story line: the beginning, the middle, and the end. Very simple. But along came Gustav Freytag, first a university lecturer and then a full-time novelist in Germany, who had the clever idea to modify Aristotle's system by adding two more elements— *rising action* and *falling action*—and to change the terms that defined beginning, middle, and end to *exposition, climax, and denouement.*

In 1863, he wrote a book, *Technique of the Drama*, which described and defined his five-part dramatic structure. This became known as Freytag's Pyramid. This is the model educators typically use to diagram Shakespeare's plays and it was the model Kaitlin was using.

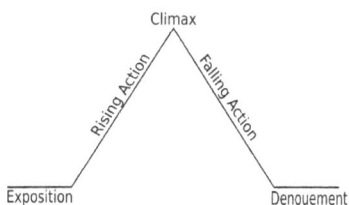

Kaitlin started. The young men were half listening. They didn't care that Kaitlin had worked really hard on this lesson. They didn't care that she was really skilled at what she was doing. They just didn't care; they couldn't be bothered. Kaitlin drew the pyramid on the board and then started to define and label the various sections of *Macbeth*. She began by talking about the *beginning* or, in Freytag's terminology, the *exposition*, while she was drawing the pyramid on the board.

147

"The beginning or exposition of the plot provides the theme and the setting of the drama and introduces the major characters. Charlie, the setting in *Macbeth* is ... ," she said waiting for a response.

"In Scotland," Charlie responded in the most detached, disinterested voice he could muster from his semi-sleep state.

"And the themes include ambition, fate, deception, treachery, witchcraft, evil, and treason," Kaitlin explained herself, not wanting to risk anyone else answering in as apathetic a tone as Charlie had. She continued, "The characters include Macbeth, a general in King Duncan's army; Malcolm, King Duncan's oldest son; King Duncan, King of Scotland; Lady Macbeth, Macbeth's wife; Banquo, also a general in King Duncan's army; ..." and on she went.

She stopped talking and wrote *Expositon* at the bottom left corner of the pyramid. Kaitlin thought the labels were important enough to use a beginning capital letter for all of them.

"Rising action," she began, and before she could say another word, the young men instantly woke up and sat up, and oh, no, I could see what was coming next and tried to send signals to Kaitlin to stop and to come to the back of the room to speak with me.

I was flailing my arms around and shaking my head from side to side trying to say, "No, Kaitlin," and "Stop, Kaitlin." She missed all my signals; she was totally engrossed in what she was doing. She continued talking. I continued flailing.

"... is an increase in tension," Kaitlin continued. And as she was talking, she was writing *Rising Action* along the left side of the pyramid.

"Oh, no, no, no, no, no." I was saying to myself. "Kaitlin, please stop and look at me," I said, still spouting to myself. I was the only one listening to me. Get ready, it was coming. There was no stopping this train.

Kaitlin reached the peak of the pyramid. She wrote and spoke *Climax* simultaneously. *Holy Mackerel!* It was done. The young men, now totally aroused (pardon the pun), were whooping and hollering, whooping and hollering, jeering and cheering. The three mortified young women in the class put their heads down on their desks and tried to protect themselves from it all by crossing their arms over their heads. Kaitlin did not know what had happened, what was happening.

Mercifully, the bell rang to end the day. The young men fled at full speed from the room, slapping each other, high-fiving each other, and laughing hysterically. Obviously, Gustav Freytag had never taught seventeen-year-old, American-male, high-school students. Otherwise, he wouldn't have fiddled with Aristotle's plan, and Kaitlin's plot diagram labels would still be something like *beginning, middle,* and *end.* Aristotle was a very wise man.

I motioned Kaitlin back to where I was sitting.

"Mrs. Page," she asked in complete disbelief, "what did I do wrong?"

"Kaitlin," I replied. "Look at the board."

She studied her own diagram for about thirty seconds; nothing. Her mind was on her lesson. Had she drawn the diagram incorrectly? Had she labeled it wrong? Her mind was not the mind of a seventeen-year-old young man who focused on the visual terms *Rising Action* and *Climax.*

"I don't get it," she said with a dubious look on her face. "It looks right to me. What did I do wrong?" she asked me again.

"Focus on the words, Kaitlin," I responded.

In another couple of seconds, she let out a shriek, "Oh no!

Oh no! Oh no!" she cried. "I want to die; I am sooooo embar-rassed," she continued. She collapsed into the seat next to me, deflated (sorry) and humiliated. It was a lesson I had learned way back in Milltown and in every school since: if teenagers can think of a sexual meaning to an ordinary word, they will. Sex beguiles and tortures adolescents. Be careful what you speak.

I doubt that Kaitlin ever used the Freytag Pyramid again. She had learned her lesson. One could hope that W. R. Grace Co. and Beatrice Food Co., whom Anne Anderson et al. had sued for poisoning the water in Woburn, had learned their lessons as well and that they wouldn't contaminate land and water again, because in 1991, the EPA, after their on-going study of the case, ordered Grace and Beatrice to pay over sixty million dollars to clean up East Woburn.

## Chapter 19

## Jackson State College, Rural Vermont, Middle Schools, and Reading in a Bathtub

What? You want me to develop teacher-preparation programs for middle schools? How do you prepare someone to teach in a rabbit hole? Do people really want to teach children who have forgotten how to walk, who trip continually, who give their friends flat tires, and who go into hysterics if a spider comes down the wall? Are men and women who want to teach in the rabbit hole as strange as the *students* in the rabbit hole? Are there adults who really want to work where things always go the wrong way? What did you say? My children will get free tuition at the University of Vermont? I accept.

And so I went to work at a small state college in Vermont way up near the Canadian border where it snows for nine months of the year; where, during the off-season, you are stuck in mud—you, your car, and the tow truck. I hadn't even completed my doctorate when I took this job as assistant professor of education. It was January and cold; twenty-below-zero-Fahrenheit cold. I learned to listen to the weather forecast every day because the reporter would tell me things like how many heating-degree days (what does that mean?) there had been in the month; whether I should venture out at all; how many minutes I could stay outside before freezing to death, which was usually five minutes or less; how long it would take my car to start, if in fact it started at all; what weather would occur in the Northeast Kingdom, and in Jericho and in Eden and in Canaan. Where was I?

I was home. And I was *at* home among nine other educators, in the College of Education, who wanted the best for school children, who wanted the best for teachers, who wanted the best for their own students at Jackson State College. And four months later, when two of the professors retired, two more came, just as dedicated, just as funny, just as proficient. I didn't care that I hadn't become a quantum physicist. Of course, I could have finished law school two years earlier and already been making a whole lot more money.

I had to learn to live with the noises of no noise. Across the street from the front of my apartment was the northern branch of the Lamoille River. There was a beautiful old, weathered, covered bridge connecting the main road in town, on which I lived, with the parallel dirt road on the other side of the river. If my windows were open, I could hear the soothing and hypnotizing sounds of the clear, clean, cold water flowing on and on over the rocks. And when it was spring and the melting snow had swelled the river, I could hear the glorious symphony of rocks moving over rocks. The music could be *accelerando* (accelerating), *acceso* (on fire), *animato* (animated), *appassionato* (passionate), *bellicose* (war-like) and then *adagio* (slow) and *tranquillo* (peaceful). I had landed in paradise. The Von Trapps thought so. After they had eluded government forces and had slipped out of Austria in the 1940s, they had settled down the road in Stowe where they managed and still manage the Von Trapp Family Lodge. If you look really hard, you can see them scampering over the hills, just as they did in Austria.

At the back of my home, what I heard were the animals that belonged to the two professors downstairs. There were the two fat pigs, Macy and Stacy, who oinked and grunted and squealed and were getting ready to be someone's Easter dinner; several beautifully soft, white sheep, looking innocent and pure, who were always bleating; a couple of cavorting goats whose bleats were more *meh-e-e* than *baa-a-a* and who spent time at the local ski resorts as lawnmowers; twenty or so egg-producing chickens clucking around; and that damn cocky rooster who crowed every morning at 4:30 a.m.

One day after I had returned from work, I heard Jim from downstairs desperately begging for help. I ran out to the back yard where he was frantically thrashing his arms around and motioning for me to follow him.

"Marilyn, please help us," he cried half choking, "Macy and Stacy have gotten out of the pen. They must be down on the road."

Jim, Stan, and I all flew as fast as we could towards the main road in front of the house. Except for that dirt road on the other side of the river, this was the one viable route in town. We went past the entry to the covered bridge and past the general store, which was the town's one commercial building. Above the store's front door was her extended, worn-out, termite-ridden sign that screeched: *Meat, Groceries, Milk, Ammunition, Deer Station.* Yes, I was definitely in Vermont. Still galloping at full speed, we continued further down the road, with me pulling up the rear. We scooted around the sharp curve, and there they were, Macy and Stacy in all their fat glory, trotting down towards the creepy, boarded-up, religious summer camp.

Have you ever tried to catch a pig? I had no idea pigs could move that fast. There were three of us, two of them; it should have been easy. But it was more like a *Keystone Cops* routine. One scurried one way, one the other. One took a sharp left into the thick brush on that side of the road; the other turned right abruptly and headed toward the river. And then Stacy was in the water, swimming. I had never seen a pig swim.

"Oink, oink, oink," came from over there. "Oink, oink, oink," came from the river. They both cried endlessly. Here an *oink*, there an *oink*, everywhere an *oink, oink, Old Mc ...* (whoops, that is another story). Jim had some kind of a collar lasso gadget and was swinging that wildly every time he got close to Stacy. I wondered how you pulled a half-ton pig in a lasso even if you did catch her. There was oinking and squealing and grunting and Jim screaming, "Stacy, Stacy, c'm here Stacy." And I could hear Stan hollering, "Macy, Macy!" on the other side of the road, deep in the bushes. Then he was whistling as if he were calling a dog. This went on and on—pig this way, human that way, pig that way, human this way. Before long, half the town center's population, which would mean about five people, had joined in the event. Everyone—Stan, Jim, I, the helpers, and Stacy and Macy—was yelling something. Watertown hadn't heard such a brouhaha for quite a while. An hour and a half later, after a lot of racing and scurrying and running and grabbing and pulling and whistling and calling, we had Stacy and Macy back in their pigpen and we were all near collapse. In case you ever want to buy a pig, just know that pigs are the Houdinis of the animal farm.

I wasn't in Inner-City 101 anymore. Now I was in Rural 101. Here the men teaching in public school weren't worrying about wearing ties, sports coats, or shoes. They were wearing L.L. Bean couture which meant red- and blue-plaid flannel shirts, heavy wool sweaters, corduroy pants, and boots. All kinds of boots: low boots, high boots, snow boots, mud boots, rain boots. And the women didn't wear high fashion either. This was all about not freezing to death. Sweaters, sweaters, and more sweaters; layered, sweaters on sweaters. There weren't any high heels clacking down the halls here. There were boots and more boots of the same variety the men wore and lots of similar corduroy, just different colors.

Socks took on a life of their own in Vermont. Everyone's boots or shoes, always muddy or snow covered or wet, got left in the home's entry way. So socks were important. At a party, it wasn't your clothes that people noticed; it was your socks. Some were funny, some beautiful. Some were plaid, some were striped, some had spiral patterns. Some beamed with smiley faces or cartoon characters, while others had gardens of flowers or mountain scenes. There were sock designs for every mood and every occasion. I came to love socks.

As different as the clothes in Vermont were from clothes in Massachusetts, the schools in Vermont stood out even more. Over the ten years that I worked at Jackson State College, I was in just about every school in the northern half of Vermont. Except for the schools near Burlington, Stowe or Montpelier, schools were typically not very big. There were plenty of schools where one building housed all grades, K–12. There were very small buildings, not as big as most houses, that contained grades K–3. And there were one-room schools that could serve as many as six grade levels with one or two students in each grade. Most of the schools were old and many were called academies, including Bellows Free Academy Fairfax, Bellows Free Academy St. Albans, Peoples (no apostrophe) Academy, and Craftsbury Academy, which gave them all an aura of gentility from another era.

But the age and appearance of the buildings belied what was going on inside. Vermont was way ahead of the rest of the country in matters of education. This was John Dewey's old stomping ground, after all. The University of Vermont was his alma mater and, since 1952, his resting place. If it was in the College of Education at the University of Massachusetts where I received the Berkeley bent, then it was this little Vermont college and the Vermont schools that put me into an educational trajectory light years out in front of anywhere else.

Judge W. Brevard Hand of Mobile, Alabama would not have been very happy here. There were no state textbook mandates in Vermont. In fact, in some Vermont schools, there wasn't any money for textbooks or workbooks at all. It was in those textbook-less schools where I witnessed the most creative learning opportunities. Did those schools hire exceptionally inventive teachers or do teachers become innovative when they can't rely on mass-produced materials?

At the K–12 Cabot School in Cabot, VT, where the employees of Cabot Cheese own the company, I found out what *progressive* and *exemplary* and *learning* really meant. The school's program reads:

> *Cabot School Philosophy of Performance-Based*
> *Teaching & Learning:*
> *Performance-based evaluation requires students to engage in time-intensive, in-depth research projects. It demands that students develop rigorous performance tasks that require students to think like historians, solve problems like mathematicians, conduct experiments the way scientists do, critically interpret works of literature, and speak and write clearly and expressively. Best of all, performance-based testing has largely been reviewed as a technique that has the potential to encompass a wider base of learning levels.*
>
> *It's great to have an encyclopedic mind, but life is not about collecting those cute little wedges in Trivial Pursuit. ... Our aim is for students to dig for depth as opposed to breadth—essentially students demonstrate a contextual understanding of their topic of study.*
>
> *The culminating exhibition is a summative evaluation; students' grades are based on the performance or demonstration of their understanding and learning. During an exhibition, assessors, parents and guests are*

*all encouraged to challenge not only the student's depth of knowledge on a subject, but how they correlate multiple concepts taught within the curriculum. Imagine an academic doctoral candidate performing a thesis defense.*

No, Dorothy, we weren't in Alabama or Texas anymore.

The Vermont I know and her schools are always moving forward. When the Carnegie Foundation released their *Turning Points* report, in 1989, the State of Vermont took their recommendations for young adolescents to heart and decided to change their junior high schools to middle schools. That didn't just mean a name change; there were substantial structural and systemic changes involved.

The *Turning Points* report recommended that middle schools, grades five to eight, replace the traditional junior high and be organized in teams of teachers and students so that the students felt they belonged somewhere; and that the teachers should hold daily advisory meetings for the students so that the students had at least one adult with whom they could address concerns, whether personal- or school-related. In addition, student discovery, problem-solving, and student goal-setting should be the foundation of the curriculum. Teachers in these new middle schools would need specific middle-school certification which focused on three critical components: theories of young adolescent development, the organization of a middle school, and approaches of student-directed learning.

Those teachers who were teaching in the seventh and eighth grades under secondary-school certification and those teaching in the fifth and sixth grades using elementary certification, all had to obtain new middle-school licensure if they wanted to keep their jobs. And new teachers had to do the same in order to get a job at a middle school. Programs had to be in place at the colleges and universities to accommodate these needs.

Our little Jackson State College received one of the Carnegie grants and I directed the effort to develop these middle-school-teacher-certification programs; not just one, but three—one for the undergraduates, one for the graduate students, and one for in-service teachers. And finally, after the Vermont State Department of Education approved the programs, here was this little college in the frigid hinterland of the north with the first middle-school, teacher-preparation programs in the Vermont State College system and offering one of the first set of programs in the nation.

Next I had to develop all the courses for the programs. First: *Young Adolescent Development.* What should pre- and in-service teachers know and understand about young adolescents? I know; they will all read *Alice's Adventures in Wonderland* and *Through the Looking Glass.* Then we will spend one, three-hour class in which they will act as their twelve-year-old selves. That should be sufficient.

Next: *Middle School Organization.* The Jackson students will be in two teams. One will act as eleven-year-olds, the other as thirteen-year-olds, and each team will complete a project. After that, each student will take a turn role-playing as a teacher responding to a twelve-year-old student's concern during his advisory time.

Last: *Middle School Curriculum.* Oh, now we are back to figuring out what curriculum is. Is it the books? Is it the sequence of courses? Is it a schedule list? If you are talking about a progressive-middle-school curriculum, it is the active and self-directed approach through which students learn; everything else, including the content, the materials, and the time-frame, follows from that. In the best of the schools, the students are the curriculum co-developers. So, of course, the Jackson students, in their middle-school-curriculum course, will produce a curriculum, based on active, discovery-learning processes, for themselves as if they were twelve-year-olds. What was it that I had said about the National History Day program back in Blackstone High School? If learning history through the NHD program does not follow the school's curriculum, then make NHD the curriculum. And there it was—NHD—a program, a curriculum, with active learning as its base. The NHD students at Blackstone had been creating their own curriculum all along. I had no idea how gifted I was.

This was just my college service work, so to speak. My real job was a four-course teaching load each semester, one course of which was supervising approximately eight to ten student teachers. I was looking forward to working with pre-service teachers once again, until I discovered that all of them were in schools at least an hour away, they were all in separate schools, and each school was at least an hour from any other. I needed to visit each student teacher eight times in a term. You can do the math. I didn't count. If I had, I never would have gotten out of bed.

I set off to visit Laurie, the student teacher at the very progressive Willton Middle School in a suburb of Burlington, VT. This school was a national model based on the new Carnegie recommendations. The Willton School Board had granted a class-free year to several teachers so that they could develop a new school program and they sure did. Not only were there grades five through eight in the school, but every class and team contained a mix of students from each grade. The parents, concerned that the eighth graders would turn their sweet and virginal fifth graders into drug addicts, pregnant ten-year-olds, and mouthy know-it-alls, had their fears put to rest. The opposite occurred. The fifth graders calmed the eighth graders down; and the eighth graders became responsible teachers for the fifth graders.

It wasn't what I thought I was going to see when I turned into the parking lot of the Willton Middle School. It looked more like a beautiful, New England home with clapboards painted carefully in a traditional, colonial white. Once inside, I walked up some stairs looking for a room or room number. There was no escalator in this school, there was no vast cavity in the middle of this building, and, in fact, there were no rooms.

At the top of the stairs in a small alcove, there was a ten-year-old boy sitting in a white, claw-foot bathtub reading a book.

"Do you get to read here often? I asked him.

"Whenever I want to," he explained.

"And who chooses the books for you to read?

"I do."

"Do you like going to school here?"

"Yes," he grinned, "it is great, way better than the school upstairs."

"What school is upstairs?" I asked.

"The regular school. They don't do anything interesting. It's really boring."

And after that conversation, I continued my search for Laurie. No, there weren't rooms here; there were areas, some with a partial partition, but most with none. In each of the areas, students were very busy, some on computers, some at tables, some at desks—all doing different things. And the teacher, who was not called a teacher at all, but a *facilitator*, was somewhere there, but it wasn't all that easy to find him.

Except for math, a class which had a regularly scheduled time, there were few formal classes here at Willton. Students learned in very different ways. If they wanted a structured class in a particular subject, they could and would ask for it and they would get it.

I eventually figured out where Laurie was and observed how she, like the facilitator, served as just that, a facilitator. She didn't get in the way of the students' learning and that is no easy thing to accomplish if you are a teacher. As I went through the school, I was asking the same questions to more of the students. And getting the same answer, "It's way better than the school upstairs."

Upstairs. Downstairs. The town of Willton allowed parents to choose between the two schools—typical, traditional grades five through eight upstairs in this building and the new, experimental middle school downstairs. Even if I hadn't asked the students, I would have known which students belonged to which school. All of the students downstairs were busy working intently on meeting the goals they had set for themselves. There wasn't a distressed, unhappy, bored face downstairs. There were engrossed, happy-looking, intent faces. No one was hanging around not knowing what to do; no one was goofing off; no one was staring out the window; no one had her head down on a desk. They had created their own goals, their own curriculum based on the school standards— which they also had a hand in developing—and on active-learning models. They knew when to ask their facilitator for assistance; otherwise they were self-educating, self-directing, self-sufficient.

There was a kiva in the center of the large area. American Indians know the kiva as a place for religious ceremonies or for communal meetings. Here at Willton, the kiva, a round area that had several rows of raised benches in a semi-circle, was used for student meetings and as a place where students could demonstrate what they had learned. I stopped and listened to a student presenting what he had prepared, scheduled, and advertised by himself. He was working on a complex science project.

Shockingly, all of the students in this downstairs school knew how to walk. I didn't see one student tripping himself or others, and I didn't see one student giving another student a sneaker-flat-tire, or anyone pushing or shoving; and I didn't see one student throwing another into a locker. Actually there were no lockers here, only cubbies. And nothing was going the wrong way.

Upstairs was a different, but familiar, world. Students sat at desks in rows and listened to teachers talking, and then they, the students, completed, ignored, or complained about worksheets and assignments. They had different faces. They looked indifferent, sad, tired, bored, and disconnected. And they were always falling down, tripping, and pushing and shoving.

It took me quite a while to get used to the new teaching-learning approach. I hadn't seen anything like this in Massachusetts, although if I had looked inside my brain, I would have found it there. That's what all the brewing and bubbly fermenting had been about. The only problem here at the experimental Willton Middle School was not here at the school; it was at Willton High School, the middle-school graduates' next stop. The teachers at the high school didn't know what to do with students who could work on their own, think for themselves, and who resisted traditional teaching. It was quite an adjustment for both students and teachers. Willton High School had not caught up with Willton Middle School.

## Chapter 20

## The Other Side of Vermont, Options, and International Travel

I loved the excuses the Jackson State College students had. They were indigenous to Vermont. Not only did they provide the reason for the late work or absences, they, in their brevity and as a composite, described life in Vermont.

*We had a chimney fire last night. (10%)*
*Our pipes froze and burst. (5%)*
*I hit a deer on the way to (or on the way home from) class. (40%)*
*I have to be away next week at sugaring camp.* (Code for: I will be cooking off the maple syrup and getting drunk next week.) *(10%)*
*I have to go to deer camp.* (Code for: I have to go hunting and I will be getting drunk.) *(10%)*
*There was no electricity in our house yesterday. (5%)*
*We weren't plowed out. (10%)*
*I was stuck in the mud. (10%)*

They were, and it was, all true. Altogether, through their explanations, the students provided me with this peculiar *précis* of life in Vermont and I think I was starting to get used to it.

Before the beginning of the next academic year, I walked down the aisle of the UMass auditorium, along with the other doctoral survivors, in full academic regalia with three thick, black-velvet, hard-earned stripes on each sleeve of the gown. Twenty fanfare, herald trumpeters at the back of the hall accompanied us to our seats. And once it was my turn to receive my diploma and I was halfway across the stage, my chairperson put the long black hood, with the crimson and white and light-blue velvet trims, which represented the university and the field of education, over my head. I had goose bumps and a jumbo-size, unremitting smile. It had been a long five years. As the president handed me my diploma, one of the drummers in the student orchestra, seated below the stage, gave me a magnificent drum roll. Thank you Jake, my son's friend. That was special.

Now that I had a doctorate, I think that meant I was a genius or a scholar or an expert at something or maybe none of those things. Nah, all it meant was that I was persistent, very, very persistent and that I had some big new words like *paradigm* and *hegemony* and *dialectic and polemic* to use whenever the opportunity arose, which turned out to be not very often.

There are doctoral programs and there are doctoral programs, and when your department consists of faculty and a dean who skipped out of the University of California Berkeley and came east, you know you are getting *progressive*. And I did. At that time there was no set program for this degree. But there were eight forms that a person had to complete to earn a doctorate. Form #1 was pretty simple; that was applying and getting accepted. Form #8—defending your dissertation—for me, was easy, because by that time, I owned my topic and research and knew substantially more than the committee members knew. Form #2, for me, was the ugly, horrible, always-winning boogeyman.

This form required that you develop your own individualized plan of study and write a rationale for the whole program. This intellectual argument basically had to answer the question, "Who cares?" I worked and I worked and I worked on that form. It was never good enough for my committee. I kept slaving and plodding and hammering away. I would write it and rewrite it, do more research, and then write it again. Finally after three years without anyone approving the form, I bought a one-of-a-kind T-shirt with the logo on the front that read: *Still on Form #2.* I wore that every time I was on campus and soon other T-shirts began appearing: *Still on Form #3* or *Still on Form #6, Damn It!* or *I Will Die of Old Age Before I Finish Form #4.* The logos started to get really creative. Somehow, this camaraderie connected to the suffering and wicked, cruel torture kept us all going. I should have opened a T-shirt store; I could have made a fortune.

It wasn't all bad. For five years I had studied tenets and effects of active-learning processes, especially in relation to adolescents, technology, and the NHD program. All I had tried to do with my junior and senior high school students; the success I had had with the NHD program at Blackstone; all the questions I had raised for myself about learning and adolescents; and everything I had already witnessed and was witnessing in the Vermont schools—it had all come together and everything now made sense wrapped up in the active-learning blanket. I had become an expert, by gum, in something after all.

Beyond that, and perhaps even more important, what this degree *did* mean was that I had options—options like teaching, directing programs, leading companies, conducting research, consulting, becoming a dean or a college president, being a school superintendent, speaking, writing, exchanging jobs with foreign faculty, and more. It wasn't what the options were that was important, it just felt powerful to have them. It doesn't make a difference what area or age of life you are talking about or who you are or aspire to be or whether you exercise them or not, it is powerful and empowering to have options.

Poverty, whose options are negligible, is the flip side of paradise in Vermont. While Vermont has beautiful scenery, water flowing over rocks in the pristine rivers, fabulous skiing, and lots of flatlanders (people who aren't originally from Vermont) who invade the state on the weekends for their recreation, it has poverty. It didn't take me long to discover these grisly pockets, the rural version of what I had seen in the inner-city schools of Massachusetts. Poverty has similar ingredients wherever you find it. And there were plenty of these among the gorgeous settings in Vermont. There was child and spousal abuse, incest, dismantled families, hunger, unemployment, health issues, drug addiction, alcoholism, robbery, rape, suicides, killings.

These elements come in all places, at all socio-economic levels, but when they are attached to poverty, you have the recipe for a place like Hardick, a town close to Jackson, which had the odious distinction of having the most incest and the most child and wife abuse in the country. There were many Hardicks in Vermont. And many of our students had their own life stories which came out of that culture. Many were first-generation college students trying to break loose from poverty's clenching fist. They wanted options.

These students carried me back to my ten-year-old self and the Saturday morning poverty-tours of my city with Dad. Here they were, the people who had lived difficult lives, who had little money, some of whom had ugly stories, exactly the group with whom I wanted to be working. Now, maybe I could actually make a difference. Not only might I be able to impact these students, but if they became teachers, exponentially, how many people could I influence through them? It was infinite. I was visualizing it and it dawned on me that maybe it was time to get a new trinket for my silver chain.

This time, how about a #1 for finally realizing I had been doing social work all along, just via a different vehicle, teaching,
and within a different field, education. Social work, sociology,
and education had all melded or melted together into an un-
noticed alliance. I guess you can't separate who you are from
what you do.

I appreciated so many things about these students. They
were not the elite, not the privileged, not the indulged, not the
well-dressed. They were the ones who had to work and fight
for everything they got. They may not have had perfect
grammar or very good writing skills, but they were not afraid
to think for themselves or speak their minds or try new
things. Whether it was surviving poverty, or absorbing the
independent spirit of Vermont, or some really amazing public-school programs, or all three, or something else entirely,
these students spoke in their own voices. They questioned
my pronouncements. Practically everything I said they challenged; they thought for themselves. Take that, Judge W. Brevard Hand of Mobile, Alabama.

We had our share of alleged lunatics as well. There was the
undergraduate who had bounced around through, and been
thrown out by, most of the Vermont State colleges and had
ended up with us. One day when we were taking a break in
our three-hour class, I returned to find all of my books, papers, and notebooks all over the floor. Shades of my class at
Woburn High School where Michael Drew had wrecked my
room, ripped up my grade book, and had ended up on the
fourth-floor ledge with my pens in his pocket. But William
was twenty-one, bigger, stronger, and crazed. His behavior in
class and his red, bleary eyes with dilated pupils made me
suspect drugs right from the beginning. He started to shriek
and wail and race around the room. I knew I wouldn't be able

to control him and hurried across the hall to the office and dialed campus security. They arrived in a minute or even more quickly than that. Three of them carted William off. I never saw him again.

There was Clayton whose writing indicated to me a current or past drug problem—the ramblings, the paranoia, the delusions, and the disconnects I had come to recognize. He was a graduate student who always carried a briefcase with him; that was a rather strange thing to carry in Vermont, in L.L. Bean country. He was in his forties and had a seven-year-old child he was not allowed to go near. In almost every class meeting, he repeated the stories to me of how the police had accused him of allegedly abusing his child and of physically harming his wife; of how he allegedly had fled to Texas; and how he supposedly had been a substitute teacher there for a couple of years. I got ill just thinking about him in a school with children.

This was also a three-hour class with a break in the middle. Every intermission, Clayton, unlike the rest of the students, stuck around in the classroom; and after telling me for the umpteenth time about his child, would ask me, "Do you want to see my guns in my briefcase?" Maybe it was a metaphor for something else, but I thought he really meant guns in his briefcase. Either way, I declined every time.

Clayton never handed in his final paper and, so, failed the class. He went on a rampage and threatened me with his guns. What exactly did that mean? He got an attorney, from the American Civil Liberties Union, who dropped him like a hot potato once she got to know him and what had happened in the class. He filed suit on his own, took his case to the Vermont, and then to the U.S., Supreme Court where all was dismissed quickly. The dean's office got involved and abruptly booted Clayton off the campus. From that point on, a security guard escorted me every night from my classroom to my car.

It was January, 1999, and while I was struggling to keep my car moving in the two-feet-deep snow, and while I was dealing with amazing, free-thinking and free-speaking co-eds on the one hand and drugged-out, demented students on the other, Hollywood and Disney had just released a new movie. It was the story of the Woburn poisoned wells, the sick children of Woburn's Pine Street neighborhood, and the trial of *Anne Anderson et al. v. W.R. Grace et al.*

The movie, *A Civil Action,* starred John Travolta, Robert Duvall, William Macy, Bruce Norris, Kathleen Quinlan, John Lithgow, and the late James Gandolfini. The movie brought the case and the plight of the people of East Woburn to national, and back to my, attention. I still worried about the people of Woburn and the students I had taught, who, by this time, would have had children of their own. Did any of my former students have leukemia? Were any of their children sick? I didn't know, but the movie reminded me of how easily an educator might become entangled in pupils' lives and how difficult it can be to forget those ties even decades later. Educators have flocks of children.

In Jackson my brood continued to grow and I continued continuing on. After living among the farm animals in Watertown for five years, I moved into Jackson to be closer to the college. I found an apartment in a converted barn, this time not across the street from the river, but right on the river. It was the same river, same sounds, only now I could sit on my back porch, which was about twelve feet above the water, put my feet up on the railing, and watch the river perpetually going somewhere.

You know when you are in Rural 101 when you have no

169

address. The U.S. Post Office would not deliver mail to me, and when UPS was bringing something to me, the address they had was: *on the river, in the barn, in the back of Woody's Appliance Store.* Speaking of which, Woody's Appliance Store was a ramshackle, old building that housed the appliance store on the first floor and an apartment on the second. There was the day I was returning from Burlington and just crossing the town line into Jackson when I saw a wide-spread, black-cloud-sort-of-thing over the whole town. This wasn't gray; this was as black as the ace of spades and didn't really look like a cloud. Whatever this huge black blob was, it just sat there.

I pulled up against my barn-home, got out of the car, and looked up at the black mess again. It looked like it was something coming from the roof of Woody's Appliance Store. I called the town health officer and it took only minutes for him, looking warm and cozy in his flannel and corduroy outfit, to arrive at my place. Health Officer Tom Blane was not young and he was missing all his top teeth. This didn't give me confidence, a health officer with no teeth; but I didn't want to be breathing whatever that black gunk was, so I had to trust that he knew what he was doing. He went into Woody's, was gone for about thirty minutes, and came back to give me the news.

"Ayup, it should be okay once this glob disappears. They were burning old, used motor oil in the fireplace to keep warm. Ayup, I didn't fine them this time, but if it happens again, I will. Ayup, give me a call if you see that black stuff again. Ayup, have a good day."

"Thanks for your help," I responded, still trying to process someone using old motor oil to keep warm. Just another day in this utopia called Vermont. All the time I had spent trying to find a place to live that didn't require kerosene for heating and here I was in this beautiful, renovated barn on the river only to be choking on burning motor oil coming from the apartment in front of me.

Vermont is a big state. The Northeast Kingdom—at first I thought that was a fake name—is a place all of its own in Vermont. Its residents regularly threaten to secede from Vermont and the United States. It snuggles up against Canada in the northeastern part of the state, hence its name. I had several student teachers placed in that area and on that Thursday, now that I could breathe again and my driveway was clear of snow, I set off on the hour-long journey. There were no GPS systems then and half of the roads weren't on any maps or even paved, As usual, there were a lot of hard-to-detect ice patches on these roads that large, snow-covered pine trees flanked. I had been traveling way too long to not have arrived at the school. Cell phones didn't work there and all I could do was drive until I found a house or a store or a sign.

Finally, I saw what looked like a little village up ahead. And just as I approached it, there was a sign over to the side and it read:

> *You are in Canada. If you did not go through the customs and border station, turn around and go back. Come back via a route with a station.*

I had no idea there were roads going into Canada with no customs station. For a split second I felt fiendishly cunning. I had gotten into Canada undetected; why not get out and roam around this cute little place. But in another second, I felt like a bandit. There were probably police helicopters or the Royal Canadian Mounted Police out searching for me. It was most likely an international manhunt already. I didn't hear any helicopters, but I would any minute. I flipped the car around and headed as fast as I could in the other direction. I only knew I was back in the United State when I saw another sign, twenty minutes later, almost the same as the one in Canada only now it said:

> *You are in the United States. If you did not go through the customs station, turn around and come back via a route with a customs station.*

Do terrorists know about these back roads? Is our country safe? And this is what I found later that day when I checked on the border-crossing web site.

> *Think twice about crossing the border at seemingly unmanned surface streets. Border officials patrol these areas constantly and use various types of surveillance to monitor streets without border stations. You have an obligation to report to a border station every time you cross the border whether it is attended or not. This is true no matter how you cross the border—walking, biking, skiing, or driving. If you are caught crossing without reporting to a border station you can face fines, jail time, and may be banned from ever crossing the border again even at a legal port.*

I was lucky I wasn't in handcuffs; I was lucky I wasn't in jail. I never crossed into Canada again.

Incidentally, I didn't find the school that day. It had gotten colder and it was late in the day; once back in the United States, I headed back to Jackson hoping to arrive home before more ice accumulated on the back roads. My visit to Shaun would have to wait for another day, a day when it was much warmer and I was much less rattled.

# Chapter 21

## A Third Catastrophe

It was an eventful year, 2001. In February, I received the news that the Vietnam Government had returned remains that they believed belonged to Allan and his co-pilot. They had found bones, dog tags, pieces of uniforms, and Allan's wallet. It would still take DNA testing to determine with certainty that they had found Allan, but it looked like he had come home. My heart skipped many beats. Allan had been missing for thirty-four years. I was a friend and I knew how I had felt over those years. I couldn't imagine what that time had been like for Allan's family. I have no idea how people who lose, or have lost family members in wars, cope.

This wasn't the only newsworthy event in 2001. As the fall semester began, I headed up to the school after watching the early morning show on TV and seeing what was apparently a small plane hitting one of the towers at the World Trade Center in New York City. That was 8:46 a.m. I had ten minutes to get to my class which began at 9 a.m., plenty of time. The college was just around the corner from my glorious barn. It took approximately one minute to get there. Some of the students were already there when I arrived; in the next few minutes, the rest all flopped in with their dripping wet hair and disheveled looks. At least they had showered.

Class began and within minutes, a student messenger came into the classroom with a notice from the main office. There were no intercoms or loudspeakers in the rooms in this old building. The note read:

*A 747 jumbo jet has crashed into the South Tower of the*
*World Trade Center. Please send any students who may*

173

*have relatives working in New York City to the office.*

There I was, for the third time, sharing a disaster with students; but this time there were some in my room who might have been directly affected. Several had family members in New York City and one had a dad who worked at one of the towers. I read the announcement and a terrible hush fell over us all. Terry gasped, jumped to her feet, and scrambled out of the room. We then knew it was *her* dad who worked in the towers.

An hour later, another student courier came into the room. This time it was the horrible news that the South Tower at the World Trade Center had collapsed and that a jet had just crashed into the Pentagon. All students were to meet in the auditorium at 11 a.m. There was chaos in my room, chaos on the campus, and the indescribable and unspeakable chaos and tragedy unfolding in New York City. Students were trying to call or receive calls on their cell phones. We all left the room and scattered to wherever we thought we would find some kind of real news. We were all wondering what had happened to Terry's Dad.

By the time we got to the auditorium, we already knew what President Barker was telling us all. American Airlines flight #11 had crashed into the North Tower at 8:46 a.m. and United Airlines flight #175 had crashed into the South Tower at 9:03 a.m. The South Tower had collapsed at 9:59 a.m. and the North Tower at 10:28 a.m., just minutes prior to the students gathering at the auditorium. We also had learned two other hijacked airplanes had crashed, the one into the Pentagon and the other into a field in Somerset County, PA. We would later learn these were American Airlines flight #77 and United Airlines flight #93.

The president cancelled classes for the day and instructed

that we keep ourselves connected to news outlets and promised that she would notify the whole campus if and when there was more news.

At this point, my accidental-career pursuit had spanned almost forty years, and three unspeakable, traumatic, national disasters had touched it. I can't ever forget where I was when I heard or saw the news, the awful, awful news. For President Kennedy's assassination, the Challenger disaster, and now this horrific tragedy in New York City, I was in front of a classroom looking at students who were looking back at me searching for some kind of direction, some kind of meaning making from me. It never came. I was as unprepared, as unable, as paralyzed, as silent as they were; after forty years in this business, I still did not know what to do. It would take several more days to hear from Terry and to learn that her father had been late to work and had survived. So many others were not so lucky.

This (2001) was my last year at Jackson. After creating the middle-school, teacher-preparation and -licensure programs; after developing and teaching over one hundred different courses; after sneaking illegally into Canada and racking up over fifty thousand miles traipsing around Vermont on my visits to student teachers; after helping to catch two run-away pigs; after listening to that cocky rooster at 4:30 a.m. about two thousand times; after several warnings from local colleagues to stay away from the Jackson Mud Bogs and from restaurants which had gun-racked trucks out front; after working with students who thankfully had and spoke in their own voices; after working with the best, the most inventive, the most supportive, the most hilarious colleagues on the planet, it was time to receive the retirement pewter bowl which wears the following engraving:

*With gratitude to*
*Marilyn L. Page*
*January 1992 – December 2001*
*Jackson State College*

# PART IV
## *DENOUEMENT*

## Chapter 22

## Not All Higher Education Is Equal: A Postscript

Two weeks later I was at my new job as faculty in the College of Education at a very large, prestigious, well-known university. I had retired, but not really; I had moved. And when you have worked with colleagues who are kind and caring and funny and intelligent and cooperative and supportive, it's a shock to find yourself in a different place where only two or three people have the time of day, where no one else cares.

Yes, I was suffering from culture trauma. First it was the lily-white town which showed off a bank, instead of a Starbucks, on almost every corner. How does this little town have enough money to support all these banks, some as big as castles, I wondered. Although it had nothing to do with the bank situation, there was something else that seemed very odd. I realized I would be teaching all of the master's and doctoral courses in a particular program. Let's just say that didn't leave much room for different points of view or much perspective in that course of study. I had questions about the town and I had misgivings about the university. Where had I landed?

Those weren't the only things I was pondering. One of the most painful discoveries was that I had moved from a relatively unknown, small state college, which had a state-of-the-art technology set-up, to a prominent university where the social-studies classroom had no technology equipment other than a WebTV that wasn't even connected to the internet. I had reversed direction. I thought I was back in 1963 at Milltown Junior High. There I was with essentially no technology and the same old, raggedy, stained, ripped, and completely out-of-date maps stacked up in the corner. I wanted to cry.

There were the students. Those in the undergraduate class were very homogeneous and very bright. Except for an odd student here or there, they all had blond hair and blue eyes. They were probably the best-looking, best-dressed students I had ever seen. They could have skipped college, passed *GO*, collected two hundred dollars, and gone straight to Hollywood to become models. They all had last names like Berker or Hartman or Werner or Clouser. I was in America Dutch Country.

If there happened to be a student with dark hair, he was always from New Jersey and had a first name like Tony or Nicky or Joey and a last name like Pagliarulo or Spagnuolo or Antanelli. He was the talker, he was the out-loud thinker, he was the one in my face about everything and anything. Most of his blond and blue-eyed counterparts rarely spoke, rarely questioned, and always did whatever I told them to do. They were ultimately the most respectful young people with whom I had worked. They were also the most repressed. I had to teach most of them to challenge me. I had to teach them how to raise critical and probative questions and to not be afraid to do it. Their anxiety about following directions exactly, *exactly*, was overwhelming. *"Color outside the lines for crying out loud,"* I wanted to shout. I wanted to shake them; maybe it would loosen them up. Each year, with each new crop of students, it took three months for them to realize that their thoughts and voices mattered and could be powerful. It took even longer for them to understand that they could do things with their voices and that, as teachers, it was not only okay, but necessary, to use them.

What had their educations or home lives been like that they

felt they could not or should not express an opinion, that they shouldn't or couldn't raise questions and invoke arguments? Is it possible for respect to go too far and cross over into blind obedience? A few weeks into the beginning of the year, I would hand out one open-ended question for the students to address:

*What is the role of a teacher in a democracy?*

Given their lack of interaction in the class, I shouldn't have been surprised at their papers. Many of these twenty-one-year-old college seniors had no idea what to write. There were scary, alarming responses:

*Teachers should be heavily involved in childcare.*
*Teachers need to make students proud of where they come from.*
*Teachers have to participate in community events.*
*They should teach about life.*
*The role of a teacher in a democracy is the same as in any other government, even a dictatorship, and that is to teach students to obey their government.*

The last is clearly the winner. Person-Up-There, give me strength.

But there were always New Jersians who, compositely, wrote about teachers preparing students to be well-informed members of society who were able to and would think; who would challenge, analyze, and question; and who would evaluate different points of view, consider different perspectives, and take action.

Thank you, New Jersey!

Yet sometimes the New Jersey delegates went a bit too far, had a bit too much spunk, a bit too much spit-fire, a bit too much bravado, a bit too much voice; and I had to rein them in. Like the time I handed Nicky back a paper with a "B" at the top. He didn't even wait for the other students to get out of the classroom when all six feet of him came charging up as close to me as possible short of bumping into me or knocking me over.

"*I have never gotten anything but an A!*" He screeched so loud he almost blew me over. I think I had saliva all over my face. "*In every grade in elementary school and every grade in high school, I got all A's!*" He screamed some more. More saliva.

I stole my response from my favorite colleague and quietly asked, "What's your point, Nicky?" as if I didn't know already.

He didn't answer; he sulked and stomped out of the room and came back a few minutes later and apologized. I have to admit that it was refreshing to have someone, anyone, for whatever reason, confront me.

Probably the biggest shock to my system at this university-with-an-attitude was the alleged old-boys' network that seemed alive and better-than-well. That Civil Rights Act of 1964 that forbade discrimination against, and promised to promote equal opportunities for, women and minorities in the workplace, ... well, the memo hadn't reached this place apparently; or, if it had, someone had misplaced it. I hadn't just gone backwards in the technology sphere or in the collegiality realm, and I hadn't just moved into a completely different kind of student domain. I had jumped into a civil-rights Pandora's box the likes of which I had never visited before—not even forty years before when I had had to sign a contract at Milltown promising not to get married.

When non-tenured women are afraid to speak in a faculty meeting, *run, ... fast.* When things are so bad that the dean feels compelled to establish a new committee to address the lack of support for, and promotion of, women and minorities, *run, ... fast.* When that meeting is making baby-steps progress and one of the alleged good-old-boys comes in during the last ten minutes of the meeting and undoes everything you have accomplished, *run, ... fast.*

That was it for me. I never attended another meeting.

A year and a half after I had arrived at this university, and while I was still trying to make sense of what I considered a treacherous quagmire, on June 4, 2003, just at the end of the academic year, the *Boston Herald* carried the news that the remains returned from Vietnam to the U.S. Government in 2001 did belong to Allan. His family were laying him to rest that afternoon in Worcester's Hope Cemetery, next to his dad. A short time after that burial, comingled remains of Allan and his co-pilot, Lieutenant Commander Donald Earl Thompson of Wellsville, New York, would be buried in Arlington National Cemetery in a single grave at Section 60, Site 8135. There really weren't then and there aren't now any meaningful words to describe what all the wondering, guessing, worrying, and feelings of loss had felt like over all those thirty-six years. That the men were back home was the only sense of relief that I or any of Allan's friends and, especially, family members would have.

To me, Allan was still eighteen-years-old; but I was not. For heaven's sakes, it had to be time to retire, for real, pretty soon. How many more programs could I develop, how many more courses could I invent and teach, how many more students could I send on their way, how many more teachers could I mint, how many more technology centers could I develop and fix, how much more research could I do? "Retire, and do what and live on what money?" I would continually ask myself. And when I couldn't answer those questions, I just kept on plodding.

And in what seemed like no time at all, it was Valentine's

Day, 2005. It was 9 a.m. and we were ready for the social-studies-methods class to begin. Suddenly, there was a knock at the back door, which was located way at the back of the room down a little, perpendicular entryway. I went back and into that hall. Only the students at the very rear of the room could see me. I opened the door, and standing there, invisible to all the students, was a young man in a black tuxedo.

"No, no no." It didn't take a second to register. "This is a stripper; this has to be a stripper. It is 9 a.m., it is Valentine's Day, and this guy is in a black tux," my mind raced. What else could it be? I had gotten used to pranks at Jackson where both students and other professors had initiated them. Although it seemed out of character at this stuffy place, it had to be a stripper. But who was the prankster? Who had set this in motion?

"Why are you here?" I asked in a distinctly unfriendly way.

"I am here for Samantha," he responded, unperturbed by my lack of welcome. "I am here to sing to Samantha."

Now I knew for sure he was a stripper, a singing stripper. I really did not know what to do. It was bad enough that it would disturb my class, but I would probably be up before the ethics board if this got around. Is there an ethics board? There must be and I would be getting a call from them.

I tried to think what to do. I needed time to deliberate. It was 9 a.m. Please! I never knew what to do in times of disasters; now I didn't know what to do about an exotic dancer, and who could think at 9 a.m. anyhow. I was a nervous wreck. I decided to leave it up to Samantha. I went back into the room and walked quietly to the front.

"Samantha, there is someone here to sing to you for Valentine's Day. Do you want him to do that?" I whispered.

"Yes, it is okay," she said quietly and a little bit shakily, as if to mean, "I guess so, but I am not totally sure." Samantha was one of the quietest students in the class.

I went back and told this tuxedoed man, "Samantha says it is okay, so you may come in." Talk about abdicating responsibility.

He came in all right and four more men followed him. They were also wearing tuxes and had apparently been hiding down the outer corridor. God have mercy. A group strip. Were they the Chippendales? Now I was really in trouble. The Ethics Board was going to find me guilty of moral turpitude. I just knew it.

The men walked to the front of the room and I think I was hyperventilating when they started to sing. They began to sing the famous doo-wop song of the 1950s, *Sh-boom (Life Could Be a Dream)* by the Chords. They started with *Hey nonny ding dong ...* , and then jumped into *Oh, Life could be a dream (sh-boom, sh-boom) ...* . It was all about two people in love going to paradise.

"So, hurry up and start taking things off," I was talking to myself, but it was meant for them, "then I will throw you out." They kept singing. They sang the second verse about plans coming true and the repeat theme about life being a dream.

"I dare you; take off your jackets!" I was still clamoring internally to myself. "No? Then whip off your pants and out you go!" I promised me. "There's something really wrong here; what are they waiting for?" my brain asked. A million possibilities were bouncing and flying from one side of my head to the other. "Are more tuxedo-adorned strippers on their way?" I asked silently. All the words were sticking in my mouth. I felt powerless.

But something else started happening; they started to sing the chorus and the class joined them, first singing along, then dancing all over the large, rectangular classroom. Before long, I too capitulated. I was dancing and singing along with the rest of the class. Who could resist that choral beat with all the *sh-booming* and *ya-da-da-ing.*

The five men finished the song. They hadn't stripped. Who were these people? What were they really here for? Had I missed something? I was confused and bewildered. And then I found out. They were the Romantics, a five member a cappella group, from the campus' singing fraternity, who roam the campus on Valentine's Day crooning in classrooms. Why had no one told me about these men?

It had been almost forty-two years since I had walked up the steps at Milltown High School, scared out of my mind, younger than young, and practicing, "Me llamo Señorita Christen." "Me llamo Señorita Christen." "Me llamo Señorita Christen," … and that choral group had to be one of the nicest, sweetest, most upbeat things that had ever happened to me, or to, or in, any of my classes. Darn, there were tears coming down my face, there were tears in the students' eyes, and Samantha was outright sobbing.

And that did it for me. All that s*h-booming* had carried me back once again to South High School in Worcester, MA in the 1950s. It was everyone's favorite song. It was one of the high-school choir's most popular songs. Once again I could see Allan singing *that* song in *that* choir. He loved music. There were so many great songs in that decade and they all had such beats that you couldn't stand still, you couldn't sit still, you had to get up and dance. You just had to dance. I knew it in the blink of an eye, in the stroke of a note—it was time to dance.

## Epilogue

Almost forty years after the landmark lawsuit of *Anne Anderson et al. v. W. R. Grace & Co. et al.*, wells G and H in Woburn remain contaminated and closed in spite of the millions of dollars the companies have already spent on cleaning up the area. No one knows, not even the EPA, whether or not Woburn residents are still exposed to the toxic brew. Woburn was one of the original sites on the Superfund, a federal list of national toxic hot spots established in 1980, and Woburn is still on the list. There has been, and continues to be, development on Woburn's contaminated lands. This includes an ice arena, hiking trails, a dog-care facility, a bus-storage yard, and an auto-supply store. Of course, the businesses don't use well water. People still live in their homes in East Woburn. Life goes on.

The Vietnam War ended thirty-eight years ago. Allan came home and received the Purple Heart, the Air Medal, the National Defense Medal, the Vietnam Service Medal, and the Vietnam Campaign Medal. His posthumous promotion made him lieutenant commander. But it seems we didn't learn very much. We still enter unwinnable wars, and now other brave men and women have come and are coming home from these new wars, in the same way as Allan did from Vietnam. They have their medals and promotions. They remain forever the age at which one last saw them. Their families and friends continue on, without them, with holes in their hearts.

Education continues much as ever, moving from one political decree to another. Different sides posture with the use of the word "reform," each meaning totally different things. There are many magnificent, innovative teachers who show up daily with their whole beings and who know when to fight and when to ignore these dictates. And there are many teachers who are unable or unwilling to stand tall, speak their voices, recognize that they have voices with which to speak, or to do what is best for children. They follow mandates blindly.

There are free-thinking states where education sometimes moves forward at rocket speed; there are other places that remain forever years behind the times. Teachers in Indiana apparently still have their very own paddles. Indiana is one of ten states in which the government protects school personnel from criminal and civil liability if they injure a student in the process of paddling. There are still nineteen states, including Indiana, that allow corporal punishment in the schools.

August 28, 2013 marked the 50th anniversary of the March on Washington for Jobs and Freedom and of Dr. Martin Luther King Jr.'s *I Have a Dream* speech. Civil rights issues still rock the nation. In June of 2013, after much mixed rhetoric from the American people, the Supreme Court ruled that same-sex couples are entitled to federal benefits; and a few weeks later, a gay-pride celebration in St. Petersburg, Florida turned violent. What will happen next in that battle?

On June 25, 2013, the U.S. Supreme Court dismantled Section 4(b) of the 1965 Voting Rights Act, which had established a federal oversight of state and local governments with a history of discrimination in voting practices. The 1965 Act prohibited these governments from implementing any changes affecting voting without first obtaining the approval of the U.S. Attorney General. Even though President George W. Bush, in 2006, had signed a twenty-five year extension of the Voting Rights Act, the Supreme Court, in June of 2013, overruled this by a five-to-four vote, and this meant that no government would be subject to this preclearance. Two months later North Carolina imposed strict photo ID requirements for voting, rolled back the early voting period, and repealed one-stop registration during early voting. Civil rights groups responded by filing lawsuits against North Carolina in federal court.

Then there came the headlines and the protests over, and the fallout and increasing polarity from, the trial of George Zimmerman who killed a black, sixteen-year-old, Trayvon Martin, allegedly in self defense. The not-guilty verdict in July, 2013, started a new racial fire. What on-going reaction, if any, will there be to this episode?

It is difficult to predict if this next news from Boston is good news or not. It may be. In April 2013, the Boston School Committee decided to throw out the last remnants of forced school busing, almost forty years after Judge Garrity had mandated it and after the *white flight* had left Boston a minority school system. Will this cause new inequities? Will whites return to the public-school system? Progress is very slow, isn't it?

The following *is* good news. The students at Wilcox County High School in the town of Abbeville, GA took things into their own hands. In April of 2013, they created their own Facebook page and gathered support for, and held, their very *first* integrated prom at the end of that month—almost fifty years after the Civil Rights Act of 1964 had outlawed racial discrimination. Leave it to the young people to get something done.

Are we on the cusp of another 1960s-style-civil-rights movement? Time will tell.

And where am I? I never saved the world. Unless there is something I don't know, I never saved a single person, unless we count Mr. Stanton who caught his tie in the uptake reel. I have no idea what my students learned from me, if anything at all. I never, ever wanted to be an educator. It was an accident of timing that I became one. I was desperate, I needed a job, there was a teacher shortage, and Milltown High School needed a teacher. It was that simple.

Now, I have finished with my accidental profession, and my brain brewery no longer deals with issues of education. I never bottled or sold a new theory of teaching and learning or of adolescent development (although, I would highly recommend attendance at the Friday night football games if you want to begin to study adolescents), because no matter what theories I came up with, they were all as old as dirt; well, at least as old as Aristotle, Socrates, and Plato. And besides, anyone can figure this all out for herself. Erik Erikson's stages of psychosocial development suggest that if older adults are able to look back on their lives with a sense of fulfilment and accomplishment, it can lead to a sense of integrity and wisdom. Does being content count?

No longer is my goal to save the world or her people. I have new things to think and dream about. My aspiration now is to learn to speak French fluently. I know this is quite a switch in direction, and I have no rational explanation, other than that I love the sound of spoken French and want to live in Paris and wake up every day smelling the bread. First, I will go to the Coeur de France Ecole de Langues in Sancerre, where in the mid-1500s, the Huguenot population held out for nearly eight months against the Catholic forces of fifteen-year-old King Francis II. I will stay in the XVI[th] century La Thaumassière château in the center of the medieval town, among all the other medieval buildings, while I become fluent in speaking French.

For two weeks, I will be studying hard at the school, living in that château with its grand, chandeliered entrance and its red wall-papered rooms with the high ceilings and its *salle de bain avec douche* and its floor-to-ceiling windows that fly open to overlook the courtyard below, and I will open those windows and pretend I am Juliet and will speak only in French, "*Roméo, Roméo, où es-tu?*"

"*Bonjour, Mademoiselle Gwendoline,*" I will say every day to my *professeur.*

"*Ca va?*" She will ask me.

"*Très bien, merci,*" I will answer.

And every day Mademoiselle Gwendoline will take me into the town center of Sancerre, which sits at the top of the hill in the gorgeous wine valley of the Loire River. We will speak only French during the ten-minute walk over the cobblestone streets and through the narrow passageways and up against the ancient buildings. Way up there, I will overlook that valley and feel like a queen once again in my new, little kingdom.

"*Combien d'enfants avez-vous?*" she will ask in our conversation.

"*J'ai deux fils et une fille,*" I will answer. "*David a quarante-trois ans et Phil a quarante-deux ans et Jeannie a trente-sept ans.*

"*Combien d'enfants avez-vous?*" I will ask *Mlle* Gwendoline.

"*J'ai un fils; il a quatre ans,* " she will respond.

"*Comment il s'appelle?*" I will want to know.

"*Il s'appelle Shaun,*" she will say proudly.

And we will arrive in town, and my task will be to buy stamps at the post office. With confidence, I will walk into *les Postes* and say what I have memorized: "*Je voudrais acheter deux timbres pour les États-Unis.*"

"*Un euro soixante-dix-huit,*" the person will say to me.

And, before I know it, I will be speaking French.

*Je donnerai au facteur deux euros et le facteur me donnera vingt-deux centimes. Et alors, nous irons à la boulangerie et j'acheterai du pain.*

*"Je voudrais acheter un pain, s'il vous plaît."*

*Et alors nous retournerons à l'école et je lirai une histoire en français et puis je répondrai aux questions que Mlle Gwendoline me pose sur Patrick et son frère et sur l' histoire.*

*Le lendemain, nous irons à la charcuterie et je dirai, "Je voudrais cinq tranches de jambon de Sancerre, s'il vous plaît," et le jambon sera si délicieux pour le dîner.*

*Et je vais prendre soin de demander les toilettes dans le restaurant; je ne vais pas demander la salle de bain. Non, non, non. Ce ne serait pas correct et la serveuse pourrait se moquer de moi.*

*Quand j'aurai terminé La Cœur de France Ecole de Langue, j'irai à Paris et je commanderai mes repas au restaurant et je prendrai des taxis et je parlerai aux chauffeurs en Français. Je serai brillante. Un jour j'irai à la Tour Eiffel et j'irai au dernier étage, et toutes les lumières s'allumeront et ce sera magique et magnifique. Oh là là!!!*

No, this is not my new dream. I should say it's not my dream anymore. This has already happened and this time it wasn't accidental; it wasn't with reluctance; it wasn't unpredictable; it wasn't equivocal; it wasn't half-hearted; it wasn't hesitant. It was deliberate and chosen and wanted and *divine*. And now, good grief, after being, and inhaling the delectable bread fumes daily, in France, I am more benevolent and practically fluent in French. Well, … getting there.

*"Puis-je avoir la prochaine danse?"* vous demandez.

*"Seulement si la danse va être à Paris."*

*Education is an admirable thing, but it is as well to remember from time to time, that nothing that is worth knowing can be taught.*

—Oscar Wilde

*A Few Maxims for the Instruction of the Over-Educated*

# List of Sources

**Prologue**
—Friedan, B. (1964). *The feminine mystique.* New York, NY: Dell; Mass paperback Edition.
—Guthrie, A. (1967). Alice's restaurant massacree. *Alice's Restaurant.* Las Vegas, NV: Reprise.
—Hornick, R. (2012). *The girls and boys of Belchertown.* Amherst, MA: University of Massachusetts Press.
—Medina, S. (2012, November 12). The smell of fresh baked bread makes us kinder to strangers says new study. *Huffington Post.* http://www.huffingtonpost.com/2012/11/02/the-smell-of-fresh-baked-n 2058480.html
—Williams, J. (1987). *Eyes on the prize.* New York, NY: Viking Penguin.

**Chapter 1. Initiation**
—United Press International. (1963, September 16). Six dead after church bombing. *The Washington Post.*

**Chapter 3. Trouble in Paradise**
—University of Rochester Medical Center. Cognitive development. *Health Encyclopedia.* http://www.urmc.rochester.edu/Encyclopedia/Content.aspx?ContentTypeID=90&ContentID=P01594
—All Free Essays. *60 free essays on cognitive development.* http://www.allfreeessays.com/topics/cognitive-development/0
—Steinbeck, J. (1962). *Travels with Charley.* New York, NY: Viking Press. (pp. 16, 57, 61, 81, 183-185)

**Chapter 4. Petitions, Persistence, and Protests**
—Collin, G. (2009). *When everything changed: The amazing journey of American women from 1960 to the present.* Boston, MA: Little Brown & Co.
—Cozzens, Liza. (1977). *The civil rights movements 1955-1965: Sit-Ins.* http://www.watson.org/~lisa/blackhistory/civilrights-55-65/sit-ins.html

**Chapter 5. Teaching on Foreign Land, Allan, and a Headache**

—Dayne, K. (2008). *The Vietnam War.* London, England: Usborn Public LTD.

—Luttrell, Martin. (2003, June 4). News: Vietnam vet's remains returned after 36 years. *Worcester Telegram & Gazette.* A1.

—*POW/MIA: Heroes of War.*
http://taskforceomegainc.org/c045.htm

—Sklarsky, C. (1967, April 29). Chicago's loud revolution: The Blackstone Rangers. *The Harvard Crimson.*
http://www.thecrimson.com/article/1967/4/29/chicagos-loud-revolution-the-blackstone-rangers/

—O'Connell, R. & Schofield, E. Jr. (Eds.). (1956). *Aftermath: The 1956 senior annual of South High School.* Stobbs Press, Inc. Worcester, MA

**Chapter 6. Boston, Tanneries, The Civil Rights Act, and Pigeons**

—Anderson, T. (2005). *The pursuit of fairness: A history of affirmative action.* New York, NY: Oxford University Press, USA.

—Collins, G. (2009). *When everything changed: The amazing journey of American women from 1960 to the present.* Boston, MA: Little Brown & Co.

—Harr, D. (1995). *A civil action.* New York, NY: Random House.

—Highhouse, S. (2012, January 11). The history corner: Was the addition of sex to Title VII a joke? Two viewpoints. *Society for Industrial and Organizational Psychology, Inc.*
http://www.siop.org/tip/jan11/12highhouse.aspx

—National Organization of Women. *The founding of NOW.*
http://www.now.org/history/the_founding.htm

—Ross, S. (2010, November 22), *Global research: Women's rights in the USA: On the amazing studies of American women.*
http://www.globalresearch.ca/women-s-rights-in-the-usa-on-the-amazing-strides-of-american-women/22046

—UCIrvine, Office of Equal Opportunity and Diversity: *A brief history of affirmative action.*

**Chapter 7. The Vietnam War, Student Differences, and the Water.**

—*Casualties—US vs NVA/VC.*

www.rjsmith.com/kia_tbl.html

—Cherlin, A. (1992). *Marriage, divorce, remarriage.* Boston, MA: Harvard University Press.

—Cover (1966, April 8). Is God dead? *Time Magazine.* http://www.time.com/time/magazine/article/0,9171,835309,00.html

—Dayne, K. (2008). *The Vietnam War.* London, England: Usborn Public LTD.

—Harr, D. (1995). *A civil action.* New York, NY: Random House.

—Motomura, A. (1998, October, 8). *A civil action: Timeline of major events.* http://faculty.stonehill.edu/amotomura/personal/lawecon/civtimeline.htm

—Vahanian, G. (1961). *The death of God: The culture of our post-Christian era.* New York, NY: George Bazillier.

**Chapter 8. Children, Three Wars, and Cerebral Cogitation**

—Arlington National Cemetery Website: *United States Navy aircrew: 4 February 1967.* http://www.arlingtoncemetery.net/aircrew-02041967.htm

—Cullen K. & Murphy, S. (2013). *Whitey Bulger: America's most wanted gangster and the manhunt that brought him to justice.* New York, NY: W.W. Norton & Co.

—Dayne, K. (2008). *The Vietnam War.* London, England: Usborn Public LTD.

—Hanchett, D. (2003, June 4). Worcester pilot killed in Vietnam finally home. *Boston Herald.* http://www.missing-in-action.com/collamore.html

—Handy, D. (2012, March 30). 40 years later, Boston looks back on busing crisis. *WBUR.* http://www.wbur.org/2012/03/30/boston-busing-crisis;

—Harr, D. (1995). *A civil action.* New York, NY: Random House.

—NPR. (2013, August 14).*'Whitey' Bulger found guilty on 31 of 32 counts.* http://www.npr.org/2013/08/12/211434280/whitey-bulger-found-guilty-on-31-of-32-counts

## Chapter 9. All Kinds of Lesson Designs and No Place to Use Them

—Citizens for Limited Taxation. *History: Every tax is a pay cut; A tax cut is a pay raise.*
http://www.cltg.org/history.htm

—Dayne, K. (2008). *The Vietnam War.* London, England: Usborn Public LTD.

—Google. *Our history in depth.*
http://www.google.com/about/company/-history/

—Hudler, G. (1998). *Magical and mischievous molds.* Princeton, NJ: Princeton University Press.

—Marcus, J. (1990). *The Jew in the medieval world: A source-book, 315-1791.* New York, NY: Hebrew Union College Press.

—Massachusetts Department of Revenue. *A primer on Proposition 2½.*
http://www.mass.gov/dor/docs/dls/publ/misc/levylimits.pdf

—Matossian, M.K. (1989). *Poisons of the past: Molds, epidemics and history.* New Haven, CT: Yale University Press.

—Nohl, J. and Clark, C.H. (2006). *The Black Death: A chronicle of the plague.* Yardley, PA: Westholmes Publishing.

## Chapter 10. Down the Rabbit Hole in Norwalk

—Carnegie Council on Adolescent Development. (1989). *Turning points: Preparing American youth for the 21st century.* New York, NY: Carnegie Corporation.

—Carroll, L. (1865, 1946, 1974). *Alice's adventures in Wonderland.* New York, NY: Grosset & Dunlap, Inc.

—Carroll, L. (1872, 1993). *Through the looking glass and what Alice found there.* New York, NY: Books of Wonder, William Morrow & Co, Inc.

—College Board. (2004). *Case study of a leukemia cluster in Woburn, Massachusetts.*
http://www.collegeboard.com/prod_downloads/yes/disease_outbreak.pdf

—History. *King Philip's War.*
http://www.history.com/topics/king-philips-war

—Marcus, J. (1990). *The Jew in the medieval world: A source-book, 315-1791.* New York, NY: Hebrew Union College Press.
—Massachusetts Department of Revenue. *A primer on Proposition 2½.*
http://www.mass.gov/dor/docs/dls/publ/misc/levylimits.pdf
—Massachusetts Department of Public Heath Bureau of Environmental Health Assessment, U.S. Centers for Disease Control and Prevention Division of Birth Defects and Developmental Disabilities, and the Massachusetts Health Research Institute. (1994). *Information booklet.*
*http://www.mass.gov/eohhs/docs/dph/environmental/investigations/woburn/woburn-summary-environmen-birth-study.pdf*
—Matossian, M.K. (1989). *Poisons of the past: Molds, epidemics and history.* New Haven, CT: Yale University Press.
—Nohl, J. and Clark, C.H. (2006). *The Black Death: A chronicle of the plague.* Yardley, PA: Westholmes Publishing.
http://www.mass.gov/eohhs/docs/dph/environmental/investigations/woburn/woburn-summary-environment-birth-study.pdf

**Chapter 12. Second Choice at Blackstone and Dynamite**
—Fuchs, M. (1996, Fall). Woburn's burden of proof: Corporate social responsibility and public health. *Journal of Under-graduate Sciences, 3,* 165-170.
—Harr, D. (1995). *A civil action.* New York, NY: Random House.
—Kennedy, D. (1998). A civil action: the real story. *Phoenix.*
http://home.comcast.net/~dkennedy56/woburn_trial.html

**Chapter 13. Ataxia and Rethinking It All**
—Collins, Gail. (2012, June 21). How Texas inflicts bad textbooks on us. *The New York Review of Books.*
http://www.nybooks.com/articles/archives/2012/jun/21/how-texas-inflicts-bad-textbooks-on-/?pagination=false
—Smith, L. (1977). *The American dream.* New York, NY: Scott, Foresman & Co.

**Chapter 14. A Deal with the Devil, a Student Teacher, and Falling Short**
—*NHD: National History Day.*

www.nhd.org

—Smith, L. (1977). *The American dream.* New York, NY: Scott, Foresman & Co.

**Chapter 15. Tragedy, Triumph, and Adolescents**

—Kennedy, D. (1998). Toxic legacy: Behind—and beyond—the hype over *A Civil Action*: A reporter revisits the scene of the real Woburn tragedy. *The Boston Phoenix.*
http://bostonphoenix.com/archive/features/98/12/17/WOBURN.html

—Kennedy, D. (1989). *Woburn toxic-waste trial: Death and justice.*
http://home.comcast.net/~dkennedy56/woburn_trial.html

—May, B, (1977). We will, we will rock you. *News of the World.* London, England: Queen.

—McDonald, A.J. and Hansen, J.R. (2012). *Truth, lies, and O-Rings: Inside the Space Shuttle Challenger disaster.* Gainesville, FL: University Press of Florida.

—Mercury, F. (1977). We are the champions. *News of the World.* London, England: Queen.

**Chapter 16. Banned Books, Criminal Vacations, and Moving On**

—Associated Press. (1987, March 18). Education: Judge amends ruling in book-banning. *New York Times.*
http://www.nytimes.com/1987/03/18/us/judge-amends-ruling-in-book-banning-case.html

—Associated Press. (1987, August 27). Ban on textbooks reversed: Appeals court rules judge too forceful on religion. *The Spokesman-Review.*
http://news.google.com/newspapers?nid=1314&dat=19870826&id=7FxWAAAAIBAJ&sjid=_e8DAAAAIBAJ&pg=5738,6982262

—Thomas B. Fordham Institute. (2004). *The mad, mad world of textbook adoption.* Washington, DC: Thomas B. Fordham Institute.

—Hartman, A. (2011, September 27). Judge W. Brevard Hand, Intellectual Historian. *US Intellectual History Blog.*
http://s-usih.org/2011/09/judge-w-brevard-hand-intellectual.html

—*Massachusetts laws: General laws of Massachusetts 6: School attendance.*

http://law.onecle.com/massachusetts/76/index.html
—PBS. John Dewey (1859-1952). *Only a Teacher.*
www.pbs.org/onlyateacher/John.html

**Chapter 18. Student Teachers, Flashback, and Those Damn Diagram Labels**

—Blackstone, J. (1988, January 10). CBS News, Immigration. *Newsmark Radio Series.*
http://newstalgia.crooksandliars.com/gordonskene/newstalgia-weekend-newsmark-immigratio#sthash.ETKnfWpA.KiLCFyCo.dpbs
—Borge, V. (1936). *Phonetic punctuation.*
https://ia700407.us.archive.org/32/items/OTRR_Victor_Borge_Coll ection_Singles/Victor_Borge_-_Phonetic_Punctuation.mp3
—Dramatic. *Wikipedia.*
http://en.wikipedia.org/wiki/-Dramatic
—Dumanoski, D. (1991, July 9). Four companies to pay $69 million for Woburn cleanup. *The Boston Globe,* p1.
—*Edmund A. Schofield.* (2010).
http://www.currentobituary.com/Memory.aspx?Memory_ObitdID= 77964
—EPA (1993). *Superfund at work: Cleanup begins at wells G and H, one year after landmark New England settlement.*
http://nepis.epa.gov/Exe/ZyNET.exe/9100580W.TXT?ZyActionD=Z yDocuent&Client=EPA&Index=1991+Thru+1994&Docs=&Query=& Time=&EndTime=&SearchMethod=1&TocRestrict=n&Toc=&TocEnt ry=&QField=&QFieldYear=&QFieldMonth=&QFieldDay=&IntQField Op=0&ExtQFieldOp=0&XmlQuery=&File=D%3A\zyfiles\Index%20 Daa\91thru94\Txt\00000022\9100580W.txt&User=ANONYMOUS &Password=anonymous&SortMethod=hMaximumDocuments=1&F uzzy_Degree=0&ImageQualiy=r75g8/r75g8/x150y150gDeree=_0& Image_Quality =r75g8/r75g8/x150y150g16/i425&Display =p|f&Def SeekPage=x&SearchBack=ZyActionL&Back=ZyActionS_&BackDesc= Results%20page&MaximumPages=1&ZyEntry=1&SeekPage= x&ZyPURL-
—Freytag, G. (1863, 2004). *Technique of the drama: An exposition of dramatic composition and art.* Honolulu, Hawaii: University Press of

the Pacific.

—*Freytag Pyramid Template*.

http://rwtverio.ncte.org/lesson_images/lesson401/freytag.jpg

—Salinger, J.D. (1991). *Catcher in the rye*. New York, NY: Little Brown and Co.

—Smith, L. (1977). *The American dream*. New York, NY: Scott Foresman & Co., 34-35.

—The Catcher in the Rye: Plot overview. *Spark Notes*.

 http://www.sparknotes.com/lit/catcher/summary.html

## Chapter 19. Jackson State College, Rural Vermont, Middle Schools, and Reading in a Bathtub

—Cabotarts. *Cabot school projects and exhibitions*.

http://cabotarts.org/projects-exhibitions/

—Carnegie Corporation. (1989). *Turning points: Preparing American youth for the 21$^{st}$ Century*. New York, NY: Carnegie Corporation of New York.

—Carroll, L. (1862, 2010). *Alice's adventures in Wonderland & through the looking-glass*. New York, NY: Bantam Classics.

## Chapter 20. The Other Side of Vermont, Options, and International Travel

—Asimow, M. (1999, February). *In toxic tort litigation, truth lies at the bottom of a bottomless pit*.

http://usf.usfca.edu/pj//articles/Civil_Action-Asimow.htm

—Ebert, R. (1999, January 8). A civil action. *Reviews*.

http://www.rogerebert.com/reviews/a-civil-action-1999

—Ezbordercrossing.com.

http://www.ezbordercrossing.com/list-of-border-crossings/    vermont / derby-line/

## Chapter 21. A Third Catastrophe

—Luttrell, M. (2003, June 4). Vietnam vet's remains returned after 36 years. *Worcester Telegram & Gazette*. A1.

—CNN.com/US. (2001, September 12). *September 11: Chronology of terror*.

http://archives.cnn.com/2001/US/09/11/chronology.attack/

## Chapter 22. Not All Higher Education Is Equal: A Post-script

—Arlington National Cemetery. Washington, DC
http://public.mapper.army.mil/ANC/ANCWeb/PublicWMV/ancWe
b.html
—The Chords. (1954). *Sh-boom (Life could be a dream)*. Los Angeles,
CA: Cat Records.
http://en.wikipedia.org/wiki/Sh-Boom
—Hanchett, D. (2003, June 4). Worcester pilot killed in Vietnam finally home. *Boston Herald.*
http://www.missing-in-action.com/collamore.html
**Epilogue**
—Amboise conspiracy. *Wikipedia.org.*
http://en.wikipedia.org/wiki/Amboise_conspiracy
—Bath, A. (2012, April 23). News: Despite opposition, paddling students allowed in 19 states. *USA Today.*
http://usatoday30.usatoday.com/news/nation/story/2012-04-
22/school-corporal-punishment/54475676/1
—Black Voices (2013). George Zimmerman poll finds divide over
not guilty verdict. *Huff Post.*
http://www.huffingtonpost.com/2013/07/17/george-zimmerman-
poll_n_3612308.html
—Cherry, K. (2013). *Erik Erikson's stages of psychosocial development.*
http://psychology.about.com/od/psychosocialtheories/a/psychoso
cial_3.htm
—*Coeur de France.*
http://www.coeurdefrance.com
—Cohen, A. (2012, April 23) *Society:* Why is paddling still allowed in
schools? *Time.*
http://ideas.time.com/2012/10/01/should-paddling-be-allowed-
in-schools/
—Editorial Board. (2013, July 21). Opinions: Equal marriages—and
now equal benefits. *The Washington Post.*
http://articles.washingtonpost.com/2013-07-
21/opinions/40713630_1_federal-benefits-federal-government-
nationalized-gay-marriage

—EPA. (2013). *Sites in reuse in Massachusetts.*
http://www.epa.gov/superfund/programs/recycle/live/region1ma
.html
—Gutman, J.M. & Curry, C. (2012, July 18). George Zimmerman wishes he didn't kill Trayvon Martin, but it was God's plan. *ABC News: ABC Nightline.*
http://abcnews.go.com/US/george-zimmerman-wishes-kill-trayvon-martin-gods-plan/story?id=16807202;
—Hirschkorn, P. (2013, August 13). Politics: North Carolina sued soon after voter ID bill signed into law. *CBS News.*
http://www.cbsnews.com/8301-250_162-57598224/n.c-sued-soon-after-voter-id-bill-signed-into-law/
—History of federal voting rights laws. *US Department of Justice.*
www.justice.gov/crt/about/vot/intro/intro_b.php
—Kilkenny, A. (2013, April 8). As Boston ends de-segregation busing, students face new inequities. *The Nation.*
http://www.thenation.com/blog/173702/boston-ends-desegregation-busing-students-face-new-inequities#-
—Liptak, A. (2013, June 25). US: Politics: Supreme Court invalidates key part of Voting Rights Act. *NY Times.*
*http://www.nytimes.com/2013/06/26/us/supreme-court-ruling.html?pagewanted=all*
—PBS NEWS HOME. (2013, August 9) The March in WA at 50: What is its relevance today? *PBS Video.*
http://video.pbs.org/video/2365061079/
—Realfancy.com (2013, July 23). Unauthorized gay pride fest turns violent.
http://www.realfarmacy.com/st-petersburg-gay-pride-fest/
—Stanglin, D. (2013, April 29). Seniors enjoy GA high school's first integrated prom. *USA Today.*
http://www.usatoday.com/story/news/nation/2013/04/29/wilcox-count-georgia-integrated-prom/2121603/
—Virtual Wall. *Philip Collamore, Jr. Lieutenant Commander.*
http://virtualwall.org/dc/CollamoreAP01a.htm
—WBUR. (2011, April 22). *The ugly truth: Mass. Superfund sites still*

*toxic nearly 30 years and more than $1B later.*
http://www.wbur.org/2011/05/22ma-superfund-sites

**Also by Marilyn L Page:**

You Can't Teach Until Everyone Is Listening

Creating and Sustaining the Constructivist Classroom (2nd Edition) (with Bruce A. Marlowe)

Creating and Sustaining the Constructivist Classroom (1st Edition) (with Bruce A. Marlowe)

Creating the Constructivist Classroom, High School Edition, Video Series (with Bruce A. Marlowe)

Creating the Constructivist Classroom, Middle School Edition, Video Series (with Bruce A. Marlowe)

Creating the Constructivist Classroom, Elementary School Edition, Video Series (with Bruce A. Marlowe)